Psychology Revivals

The Psychology of Misconduct, Vice, and Crime

Born in Vienna in 1864, Bernard Hollander was a London-based psychiatrist in the early twentieth century. He is best known for being one of the main proponents of the interest in phrenology at that time. This title, originally published in 1922 contains the reflections of the author on his experience as a physician specialising in nervous and mental disorders. He looks at a range of patients "suffering from character defects leading to moral failings..." finding that these cases of "moral derangement" come in all kinds. Very much of its time, he suggests that treating the causes should be with both physical and mental measures, including psychotherapy, which at the time consisted of "persuasion, suggestion, auto-suggestion, hypnotism, psychological analysis, as well as re-education." A fascinating glimpse into psychology from the early twentieth century.

The Psychology of Misconduct, Vice, and Crime

Bernard Hollander

Routledge
Taylor & Francis Group
LONDON AND NEW YORK

First published in 1922
by George Allen & Unwin Ltd

This edition first published in 2015 by Routledge
27 Church Road, Hove BN3 2FA

and by Routledge
711 Third Avenue, New York, NY 10017

Routledge is an imprint of the Taylor & Francis Group, an informa business

Publisher's Note
The publisher has gone to great lengths to ensure the quality of this reprint but points out that some imperfections in the original copies may be apparent.

Disclaimer
The publisher has made every effort to trace copyright holders and welcomes correspondence from those they have been unable to contact.

A Library of Congress record exists under LCCN: 23006417

ISBN: 978-1-138-84149-9 (hbk)
ISBN: 978-1-315-73216-9 (ebk)

THE PSYCHOLOGY OF MISCONDUCT, VICE, AND CRIME

BY THE SAME AUTHOR

MENTAL FUNCTIONS OF THE BRAIN

MENTAL SYMPTOMS OF BRAIN DISEASE

FIRST SIGNS OF INSANITY

THE PSYCHOLOGY OF MISCONDUCT, VICE AND CRIME

Some Reviews of the First Edition

"It is unusual in these days to find an eminent mental specialist producing a book upon his subject in a language that proves intelligible and extraordinarily interesting to the ordinary reader."—*Westminster Gazette.*

"A great deal more enthralling than almost any novel . . . above all it is extraordinarily human."—*Time and Tide.*

"Dr. Hollander's book, indeed, affords one of the clearest, simplest, and most concise accounts of the motives of human action that could be placed in the hands of one unfamiliar with the Freudian and post-Freudian doctrines."—*Nation.*

THE PSYCHOLOGY OF MISCONDUCT, VICE, AND CRIME

BY

BERNARD HOLLANDER, M.D.

LATE PHYSICIAN BRITISH HOSPITAL FOR MENTAL DISORDERS AND NERVOUS DISEASES; HON. MEMBER ROYAL ACADEMY OF MEDICINE, MADRID

LONDON: GEORGE ALLEN & UNWIN LTD
RUSKIN HOUSE, 40 MUSEUM STREET, W.C.1
NEW YORK: THE MACMILLAN COMPANY

First published . . . September 1922
Second Impression . . January 1924
Third Impression . . February 1928

Printed in Great Britain by Phototype Limited, Barnet, Herts.

PREFACE

In the course of twenty-five years' practice as a physician specialising in nervous and mental disorders a large number of people have come under my observation and treatment, suffering from character defects leading to moral failings—some complaining of a tendency to misconduct, which remained a tendency only; others being brought to me for the evil they had already committed, doing harm to themselves or to others. Some of these were addicted to the drink or drug habit, some to sexual perversion, some to ill-temper and violence; while others were youthful liars, thieves, or profligates. Finally, a considerable number consisted of semi-insane and semi-responsible young men and women, morally deficient—sometimes together with mental defect; sometimes mentally so superior, at least in cunning and conversational gifts, as to be admired by everyone with whom they came into contact, until found out. It will be seen, therefore, that the cases of moral derangement which come before the mental specialist are of all kinds; only the professional thief and burglar, and the downright scoundrel, do not consult the physician.

This book contains the results of my reflections on these experiences. It is written from the standpoint of the "new psychology," dealing successively, in accordance with their evolution, with the primary emotions and instinctive tendencies which are at the basis of all human behaviour, normal and abnormal. Of course, there exists already a vast literature on Crime and Criminals; but I know of no book which presents systematically, in their medical and psychological aspects, the various divergencies from normal conduct with which the mental specialist has to deal, with the possible exception of W. Healy's important work on *The Individual Delinquent*, which treats the subject from a different point of view.

It will be shown that morality is a gradual growth, arising from the conflict between the unconscious instinctive tendencies to self-gratification and self-preservation, and the gregarious instinct which produces in man the various affections, parental, filial, and social, and ultimately tends to altruistic conduct. Some people are naturally moral, some are inherently selfish, and others—perhaps the great majority—are conscious of the two tendencies within them, and remain moral under temptation solely from fear of consequences. The morally deranged can be distinguished from the professional criminal class by the lack of self-control. They are conscious of thoughts and impulses towards evil-doing which they desire to inhibit, but lack the power to do so.

They come to the physician to do for them what they cannot do for themselves. In the actual criminal there is no conflict ; he " wills " to do wrong. It is the business of the doctor to reform the former ; it is the business of the law to punish the latter.

In judging a moral patient we have to take into account his heredity, environment, and early education, as well as any possible disorder or defect of the brain, and the nutrition and circulation, on which its proper functioning depend. It is this, the physical basis of morality, which is so often neglected, chiefly because most men lack a theory of what constitutes a good brain or a bad one. This problem of the relation of the brain to mind and morals has been investigated by me and dealt with in my earlier works, *The Mental Functions of the Brain, Mental Symptoms of Brain Disease, First Signs of Insanity,* and more fully in my recent publication entitled *In Search of the Soul* (Kegan Paul, 2 vols.). In the present book I shall deal chiefly with abnormalities of moral manifestation from a psychological and common-sense point of view, free from any preconceived theory.

Just as we have to investigate abnormal conduct physically as well as mentally, so must the treatment be by physical measures as well as by mental influences. On the one hand we must raise the tone of the brain and nervous system, and correct any constitutional defect or brain lesion ; on the other we must give relief along sound scientific lines of insight into the mental mechanisms which underlie moral troubles and assist the sufferers to a more effective adaptation to the demands of life. Such psychotherapy consists of various methods—persuasion, suggestion and auto-suggestion, hypnotism, psychological analysis, as well as re-education. There are practitioners for each, but I have not found that such specialising produces satisfactory or lasting results, and therefore, as a rule, make use of the method, or combined methods, most applicable to the individual needs of the patient.

BERNARD HOLLANDER, M.D.

57 Wimpole Street, London, W.1.
1st *May*, 1922.

CONTENTS

Will the reader please note that the description of the Freudian theory of complexes (Chapter I, pages 24–27) is largely made up of passages from the well-known standard work on "The Psychology of Insanity," by Dr. Bernard Hart, and that the author regrets very much that inadvertently no indication was given of their being quotations and their source.

The Psychology of Misconduct

CHAPTER I

THE PSYCHOLOGICAL BASIS OF MISCONDUCT

PSYCHOLOGY is not merely the science of mind, mainly concerned with the analysis of consciousness by the method of introspection, but is also the science of behaviour, whose subject-matter is conduct and must be studied individually in its biological, social, and environmental connections. Psychology, as now understood, is an immensely practical subject and deals with the problems we all have to face in our own lives. Without a study of the human mind and the psycho-physical forces which produce conduct, it is impossible to understand the origins of misconduct.

It may not be pleasing to human conceit, but there are a number of elementary instincts and feelings, which we possess in common with animals, which are aroused spontaneously, and are implanted by nature for the preservation of the individual and the race. These instincts in man do not act blindly as in animals. They are reduced in him to obscure impulses which urge him in certain directions, but leave him to choose the itinerary of his course. Instincts, in man, therefore, are sometimes spoken of as *propensities.* These propensities are simply rudimentary impulses, which make us want to act in certain ways under certain conditions, and are not acquired by the individual, but are transmitted in the germ from generation to generation. They act powerfully of themselves; whereas the rational faculties require to be cultivated, exercised, and to be instructed. The propensities give force to the character; the intellect shows the means of directing that force; and the higher sentiments, which are the special prerogative of man, suggest impersonal uses of that force. Without the propensities and the feelings to which they give rise there would be no stimulus to the exercise of the intellect, for the intellect can appreciate facts but does not supply motives; and in judging a man we have to ask what are the motives which habitually determine his conduct, whatever be the means his intellect may devise for the attainment of his ends. All propensities have a good purpose; only when wrongly directed do they become vicious. On their activity depends all the good and evil in life.

There is one group of propensities whose primary function, in animals and man alike, is the *preservation of self.* In order to maintain existence, both animal and man must possess the *combative propensity.* They must destroy or kill for food; they must also be alive to and able to remove the dangers by which they are surrounded; they must be capable of *resentment* also, in order to prevent themselves from being destroyed and be capable of inflicting injury on their foes. These actions are absolutely needful for the preservation of the individual. In civilised human beings this disposition manifests itself in a greatly modified and altered manner, because of our great civil organisation, which in place of teeth and claws has made money, by reason of its purchasing power, the chief protector of life.

The combative propensity and propensity of resentment are accompanied and aroused by a special emotion—that of irascibility or anger, which gives strength for the fight by increasing the physical energy. That the sight of one's foes should cause irascibility and in extreme cases rage, is a reflex mechanism of immense preservative value in the struggle for existence, for thereby muscular changes are developed spontaneously all over the body and the strength of every muscle is exalted. When we get angry, the spontaneous impulse is to inflict injury on the originating cause. But this aggressive propensity can be active also without anger. It gives to the character its executive energy, without which no undertaking can be successful.

Animals having constantly to safeguard themselves against their numerous enemies, to prevent their being themselves devoured, have developed a tendency to concealment, which has also proved useful in approaching their prey. This has given rise to the feeling of *suspicion.* When we see a strange being or object, curiosity is aroused; but if very strange—suspicion. Suspicion is a protective instinct and consequently a necessary quality. Every grade of suspicion prevails among human beings, and may lead to secretiveness. While some are disposed to be open, straightforward, and outspoken in their manner, probably from the long protection within society, others, more egoistic, practise falsehood and deceit.

Some animals are not equipped for fight, and in them is aroused the emotion of *fear,* especially at the sight of something strange. Fear sounds the trumpet-note of danger and leads the animal to seek safety in flight, or else to hide, or to sham death. Fear is an innate disposition to self-preservation. With little fear there is often little caution, and the danger is not seen until escape is impossible. Courage frequently means blindness to danger, a lack of imagination to realise the horrors of a distant catastrophe.

Certain zoologists have argued recently that fear is not an innate but an acquired emotion, because young animals approach their enemies without signs of fear. But this is simply because the young animal does not yet recognise its enemy. For children too will approach a fire, and even a lion, without fear, simply from knowing no better; but fear is innate all the same, though it varies in degree in different individuals.

Some animals found it useful not to hunt continuously for food, which may prove scarce at certain periods, and began to store up things for future use. Thus developed the ***hoarding instinct***, a tendency to lay up provisions for the future. Man not only stores up provisions for winter, but he acquires property of every sort and kind for all his life and for his posterity. He does so not only for the joy of building up possessions, but also because it enables him to gratify ambitions and gain social esteem. The acquisitive propensity varies in different people ; the ability to acquire depends on the intellect and other requisite qualities. It imparts the love of possession.

Besides these propensities, which are for the most part essentially egoistic, there is the ***sexual propensity***, which, though followed for personal gratification, tends to propagate the species. The gregarious instinct in man has developed also a certain number of feelings which attach him to his kind and certain dispositions whichgive him the power of adaptation to his fellow-men, whose approval or disapproval influence his conduct. From the pressure of social life developed altruism.

We possess, then, two groups of mental qualities : one destined to preserve the individual, the other to preserve the race. Both make us follow certain paths of life ; but we are not following them because they serve a definite and ordained end in nature, but because their satisfaction is accompanied by a pleasurable feeling.

Thus, the animal is aware of the sensation of hunger and experiences appropriate pleasure from the food its taste approves of ; but it has no knowledge that the assimilation of new material is an indispensable necessity in the maintenance of animal life. Like the animals, so do we do innumerable things to which we are led by purely organic impulse ; things which indeed have a reason and a use, but a reason which we never know, and a use which we never discern, till we come to think. A man is tender, hard, credulous, cynical or benevolent as a result of the predominance of one or more innate qualities which turn the scale in that direction, and, whatever his disposition, he derives gratification from following it. The greater the strength and activity of a mental quality, the greater the pleasure attending its exercise.

If the passion of love is strong in us, we think we have decided to love ; whereas our organisation has rendered us more liable to be stimulated by such external impressions as would arouse love. Any of the primary emotions and propensities may be so strong as to render any balancing of the ends in view out of the question. The man agitated by jealousy and the desire for revenge considers himself a free agent so long as he feels satisfaction from the achievement of his desires. When the storm calms down, he changes his tone, and acknowledges that he was carried away by the impulse of his passion. After the event, total contradiction is manifested between the natural sentiments and the act committed, and this contradiction is what constitutes repentance, or the natural conscience. The prayer "Lead us not into temptation" in a certain sense implies that the individual is afraid of his own desires. We often hear it said that a certain man is his own worst enemy, which means that his welfare is menaced, as through a hostile influence, by wishes that are really his own. Temptations may be removed, yet the desires persist. Temptation is therefore the presentation of opportunity to satisfy desire. Misconduct is due to temptation or opportunity (the environmental factor or stress) acting upon the predisposition of the offender (the inherent or constitutional factor).

Everyone acts according to his own disposition, but those deeds are most praiseworthy which are for the good of the greatest number.

The mental constitution of man consists of animal propensities, social feelings, egoistic sentiments, intellectual capacities, ethical and so-called religious sentiments. All these vary in degree of strength in each individual. We find, then, that man is possessed by a variety of mental powers, which have different functions to perform, different duties to discharge, and between which there obtain certain relations and connections, some ranking higher, some lower, yet all useful and necessary in their proper place. These primary mental powers exist in all men; their difference is one of degree only. One has more apprehension and less aggressiveness, more self-reliance and less veneration, more affection and less greed, than another. We start life unequally because of the difference in our inherent proclivities and the difference in our surrounding circumstances. Education, law, public opinion, tend to repress impulses and to produce uniform conduct; but nature will out. That our dispositions are innate, and not the result of education and training, is evident from the contrasts which we observe between members of the same family. Let wealth and power be distributed as you will, the more industrious, the more artful, and the more gifted men will have the best chance to rise to superiority. Only the animal is contented, at least so long as it gets its food. Man rarely ever is contented; he desires possessions, power, influence. Our innate dispositions give us realisable potentiality, and environment makes the realisation of potentiality possible. There are many geniuses in the world who remain undeveloped and obscure for lack of opportunity; there are many imbeciles whose defects are hidden because they are never called upon to do anything requiring intelligence; and there are many criminals in the world who remain honest solely because they have never been subjected to temptation.

The propensities supply the dynamic energies to

human conduct, and we can no more do without them than without our senses. In some they control the reason; in others, the more perfect, they are controlled by the reason. The thoughts are often merely the expression of predominating emotions and propensities; for example, thoughts of sex in a sensuous man on the approach of an attractive female, thoughts of business in the greedy man on a favourable opportunity, thoughts of infidelity in a jealous person on the slightest suspicious circumstance, and so forth. We imagine that we ordain the direction of these thoughts, whereas very often we are only following them. The moral person may have thoughts of misdeeds, but he does not dwell on them; whereas the immoral person "contemplates" mischief.

The intellect may be highly developed, and the emotions and propensities very ill developed, or the reverse. The fool may have a kind and affectionate heart, and the criminal a quick wit. Of course, intellectual and moral defects may also coexist. Were intellect not entirely distinct from emotion and propensity, the complete idiot would also be incapable of manifesting them; whereas, on the contrary, the emotions and propensities are manifested the more strongly for lack of the inhibitory control of reason. The impulsive force of the propensity is able to traverse his desert brain without obstacle.

The primitive propensities which prompt man

do not manifest themselves in the same rude and open manner as they do in animals, owing to the training we receive. The education of the infant and child consists not only of the drawing out of their intellectual abilities, but to a much larger extent of the repression of their instinctive impulses. Later, other restraining forces come into play, such as family ties, public opinion, communal interests, and especially the activity of the understanding. The fear of consequences and the desire to please others are the strongest forces to inhibit our desires. The fear of exposure, trial and punishment has restrained many a man. The shame, too, that would be brought on his family and those that are dear to him, helps to keep a man moral. If he is instinctively afraid of being found out in wrong-doing, he will live a faultless life, just as truly as his neighbour who obeys the laws from a moral conviction.

Moral conduct is conduct that serves the common interest. We accept those things as right that are generally approved; and many people never go beyond this stage. They accept the conventional morality that they find prevalent, and repress their personal instincts in order to comply with the wishes and ordained customs of their fellows. Their judgment of what is right is based on the approval of others. In the struggle for existence among men, it is not the fittest that survive, but those who most readily adapt themselves. "The conscience that makes cowards of us all" is largely our desire for the good-will and appreciation of our fellow-men. The public punishments of the whipping-post, the stocks, and the shameful exposure on the pillory to public scorn and abuse, and still more the terror of the scaffold when executions were public, were primitive measures employed formerly to teach social responsibility.

Right acting, however, does not necessarily mean right thinking. The highest conduct is dictated, not by the desire to secure approval and avoid punishment, but by the simple desire to do what is right because it is felt and believed to be right; in short, from a sense of duty. Therefore it must be spontaneous.

Most evil-doing springs not from anything wrong in the original and primal desire, but from the imperfection of the higher and superadded elements in our nature. It will depend on the early education whether the primal tendencies retain their original energy or are transformed. If the propensities for self-preservation are untutored, they are pursued for their own sake, as an end in itself—the food instinct in the gourmand, the sex instinct in the Don Juan, the acquisitive propensity in the money-grabbing man—and they become, from the ethical standpoint, vices. The innateness of the propensities is shown in certain states of clouded consciousness and in brain disease, when they manifest themselves in their full vigour and in the coarsest manner.

Because of this untutored manifestation, the propensities have been called evil or immoral; but they are simply non-moral. For only out of action can morality be evolved, and only by desire can primitive man be spurred into action. The greater the intellect of a man, the greater the check upon his emotions and passions. The lower the power of the intellect, the more freely do the feelings and propensities influence the actions of the individual. Therefore a child, a savage, and persons of little culture, are little able to restrain their inclinations. In low-grade surroundings exhibitions of low passions are often applauded, language is coarser and more inciting; consequently the frequency of transgression, deadly fights, sexual assaults, etc. But reason is not the actual controlling force. It has that power only by exciting a higher feeling to suppress the lower, so that the struggle is, as a rule, between feelings, and not between reason and feeling. The impulse is first aroused, and the intellect steps in afterwards. Therefore, where there are no higher faculties to be called up, the intellect will simply act in the service of the lower ones.

All our dispositions, those derived from our instincts as well as those due to habits, are unconscious. Only after their manifestation do we become aware of them. It is only on reflection that most men realise the motive which prompted them to certain conduct. But though the motives arise from the unconscious, the acts to which they prompt are executed consciously, in normal men. Therefore, when a person says, "I did it unconsciously," he does not mean that he was unconscious when he did it; he means that he did it without paying any attention to the action. It is on account of our unconscious dispositions that we see the world through different spectacles and the scenery suggests to us different ideas. Much of human conduct, both normal and abnormal, proceeds, not from consciously reasoned motives nor from any chain of association of clear ideas, but from the great compelling forces of the unconscious propensities that work within us. The impulses they give rise to frequently are opposed to our conscious desires, the conventions of education and experience, and our general views and principles; and if this conflict in the mind below the threshold of consciousness is not inhibited, disordered conduct may result. This is an old truth—known as the struggle between the flesh and the spirit—which has been revived by modern psychologists and explained as the conflict between mental complexes and the personality.

Complexes are formed by the interaction of our inherited emotions and propensities with our thoughts and the impressions constantly flowing in from the external world. Once formed, a complex limits and determines the modes of expression of the instinct and makes us accept ideas and arguments which are in harmony with it; whereas those not so in harmony tend to be inhibited. Prejudices may be thus explained. Consciousness is rarely permitted to approach a new matter without subconscious prepossessions. It is overruled—or guided, as the case may be—by what has gone before. In accordance with the complexes already formed, so will "suggestions" appeal to us and we shall be influenced by them. The person with an open mind, i.e. with fewer compact or dissociated complexes, is more likely to use his judgment in appeals that are made to him through his senses. When a complex consists of painful experiences or is for some reason out of harmony with the remainder of the personality, it is "repressed"; that is, thrown out of action and banished from the conscious mind. It cannot enter consciousness any longer without resistance, but, though apparently forgotten, it still exists and exercises a distorted influence, or may become completely dissociated. That is how obsessions may arise. Much of the "forgetting" which occurs in our lives is not the passive process of decay which it is commonly supposed to be, but an active repression, a deliberate exclusion of the offensive memory from the sphere of consciousness.

Another way of finding a compromise between the opposing groups of ideas of complex and personality consists in the expedient of preserving both, while at the same time all contact or interaction between them is sedulously avoided. By this means the man whose morality in private life is unimpeachable is enabled to practise a quite different moral code so far as his commercial transactions are concerned, because the two spheres of action are kept rigidly separate in his mind. The man whose commercial morality differs fundamentally from the code which he practises in his private life, persuades himself that the latter code is not properly applicable to business relations, that to ask a customer three times the value of an article is obviously something quite different from thieving, that a man must live, and that the immorality of lying completely disappears when it is necessary for the support of one's wife and family.

We cannot repress all our complexes; and those our better nature does not approve of, or we are unable to repress, we try to explain to ourselves by the manufacture of plausible reasons, more agreeable and acceptable to us than would be a correct understanding of the real motive force. We are always excusing our conduct, whether in private or in public life. We are all constantly inventing reasons in defence of our interests and inborn character, giving way to conscious or unconscious hypocrisy. This process of self-deception in which the individual conceals the real foundation of his thoughts by a series of adventitious props, is termed "rationalisation."

The mechanism of rationalisation is most evident, perhaps, in the sphere of moral conduct where we tend always to ascribe our actions to a conscious application of certain rules of life and ethical principles, enforced upon us by the community as a whole. Thus it is a familiar fact that people of otherwise irreproachable honesty will swindle the Government or a railway company with untroubled equanimity. If they are taxed with the incongruity between their principles and their conduct, a varied crop of rationalisations will be immediately produced. They will point out that a company is not the same thing as an individual, that nobody really loses anything, that the fares or taxes are so inequitable that it is justifiable to evade them, and so on.

There is still another method by which we try to conquer our disagreeable impulses and unapproved complexes. This is by so intensely occupying ourselves with other matters of a widely different and, if possible, higher nature, that no time is left for the impulse to arise. This is called the process of "sublimation," and is perhaps the best way of escape.

When a desire arises in our mind, it may pass at once into action; but usually reflection is aroused at the same time and we weigh the consequences of gratifying our impulses. To this act of determination we give the name of *volition.*

Volition is determined by two factors: the external circumstances by which a man is at any moment surrounded, and the various desires and thoughts excited by them in the man himself. In our full consciousness we act as we choose, but our choice is usually determined by our character, i.e. by those dispositions which we inherited and follow habitually. We can control our innate desires and innate dispositions, but we cannot eradicate them. The men with the character of a lamb, or the character of a fox, are described as such because of their habitual conduct. We can change only by making repeated conscious efforts. Unconsciously we act according to the strongest motive. Consciously we can choose—not the motive, but among the motives. And although the strongest motive will have the greatest attraction for us, we can act contrary to it. We are not compelled to do anything.

When there is only a single and immediate motive, we term it an *impulse.* The greater the variety of motives, the more hesitancy in action. Doubtless some persons are less tolerant of explosive energy—as that of anger, for example—than are others, and these are the people who are naturally very impulsive. In others there is a greater possibility of radiation into surrounding associations by which the explosiveness and the emotional tone are dissipated. Everything which checks impulse must be regarded as moralising.

Most men would feel a strong impulse to kill a man who had unjustly attempted to destroy their family life or moral reputation. This would be a psychical cause; but men may act impulsively also from physical causes, such as a sudden rush of blood to the brain, or intoxication by alcohol.

The will is often powerless, even in the best of us. We are all haunted at times by certain ideas or memories of past experience. We may by change of topic, association, fresh impressions, get rid of some troublesome idea; but to dismiss it at once by an effort of will is often beyond our power.

It is the man with the greatest choice of motives, the man whose mind is cultivated and in whom the social and ethical sentiments predominate over all selfish desires, who enjoys the greatest freedom, and whose conduct can be least determined. The less a man is educated and the lower his organisation, the fewer motives will he have, and the more easily can his actions be predicted.

The will which is swayed entirely by low motives is less free than that swayed by higher motives. Consequently, when a person is blamed for having done ill, he is not blamed for not having acted without motives, but for not having been actuated by the highest motives. Moral reprobation attaches, not to the bare act, but to the balance of motives to which the act is an index.

Will is not only the power to act, but also the power to restrain. Self-control has to be learned, not only to divert energy into higher channels, but in the interest of the community of which the individual forms part. Some people never acquire inhibitive control; others possessed it but lost it, or temporarily lose it. Strength of will is not always real strength; nor weakness of will, real weakness. Many a weak-willed man has made gigantic efforts to suppress his will; and the so-called "iron-will" is often only a mask of strength cleverly assumed by weakness. The secret of success is to will what one is able to do, and to be able to do what one wills.

Most crime that is not professional is due to the failure of inhibitory control, the inability to refrain from the satisfying of some strong instinct, though such satisfaction does not meet with the approval of the community and is therefore considered immoral, or though such satisfaction conflicts with the legal standards of conduct. The failure may be due to the impulse being unduly strong or the power that should control and direct it being unduly weak. These two factors, strength of propensity and counteracting motives which give power of inhibition, are constantly varying in each individual under the influence of the innumerable and complex conditions of social life.

Some people never rise much above their propensities, resembling animals as regards the life they lead. Others, though endowed with considerable intellect, still have not enough of it to resist their propensities. Repeated yielding to impulses creates a habit of self-indulgence; repeated resistance builds up a habit of self-control. Indulgence being easier than resistance, bad habits are more easily contracted than good habits. The crimes and follies of mankind are mainly due to the uncontrolled operation of the propensities. The best of us lack control sometimes. Not that we do not know right from wrong, which even many insane persons can distinguish; but very few people can resist temptation, if the temptation be sufficiently strong. Even fear of punishment is not a sufficient deterrent; because most men in yielding do not reckon with it, but are inspired by the hope of not being found out. Of course, where the desires never have been strong or have faded with age, it is easy to be moral; but there can be no virtue where there is no desire, and consequently no temptation. The impulses of mankind are probably as strong to-day as they were in prehistoric times; but civilised life has created society on a large scale, and no society can exist where moral laws are not observed. Morality consists largely in a compact with our fellows to live with them on the best possible terms. It is an agreement not to kill one another, not to steal from each other, not to lie to or about each other.

The mistake is often made of attributing moral transgressions entirely to impairment of will, as if man were instinctively moral in tendency and, when he does not follow his moral impulses, simply lacks the will to follow them. This is a serious mistake. Moral obliquity may be the result of personal volition. The will to commit breaches of social ethics may be as strong in one individual as the will not to commit them is in another. Right acting, indeed, may require no effort of the will whatever. It may be, and perhaps usually is, automatism built up from a well-developed conscience and moral sense, with no conscious effort in its application. The power of temptation is, of course, greatest in those with strong animal instincts and poorly developed mental powers of that kind which give the power of inhibition.

Consequently we can draw no definite line of demarcation between those who are moral and those who are immoral in their actions; and to understand the reasons for misconduct we must know the innate dispositions, acquired habits, and the force of the mental complexes of the offender. Anyhow, the efficient causes will not be those lying upon the surface, but deeper processes, only to be unravelled by a delicate psychological analysis.

CHAPTER II

THE CAUSES OF MISCONDUCT

WE have explained in the preceding chapter that man inherits certain deeply ingrained propensities to action from his remote past which are for the most part essentially egoistic and come in conflict with his gregarious instinct and the altruistic sentiments arising from it. In consequence, in course of time, standards were set up and laws made for the regulation of conduct and the person who violates these standards or fails to conform to them is considered immoral, and if against the law a criminal. It has also been explained that, in most cases, the fundamental impulses concerned in moral failings have nothing specifically immoral in them; that they are essentially the same impulses and aptitudes that come into play in strictly moral conduct. For example, the acquisitive instinct can be exercised morally or immorally; so can the sex instinct and other instincts. Indeed, vice is frequently only virtue in excess; as when prudence turns into cowardice, courage into rashness, economy into avarice, liberality into prodigality, liberty into licence, submission into slavery, pride into conceit, love of approbation into vanity, and constancy into obstinacy. Conduct, therefore, may be immoral, but there are no immoral mental qualities or dispositions. Only that conduct is immoral which, if every one did it, would be detrimental or destructive to society. The vast majority of moral offences are of a private character; that is to say, are hurtful to individuals only. Still, some of them are looked upon with peculiar abhorrence and punished with great severity, though they may injure no one. These are the sexual crimes and unnatural offences.

It has further been shown that most normal persons are potential moral offenders and law-breakers, for the primitive propensities are common to all mankind. They are, however, not actually immoral, inasmuch as they have developed in addition certain inhibitory qualities which enable them to modify and restrain these impulses in accordance with the standards of their society. Whether a man becomes a moral offender or not depends on the strength of the temptation to which he is subjected and on the strength of his moral motives to withstand the temptation. Very few people would resist temptation if the temptation were sufficiently strong. It is easy to be virtuous when one happens to be so organised that one has no inclination and when one has never been tempted;

but a born eunuch deserves no credit for being a celibate.

Human beings are to a large extent the victims of their organisation, partly inherited from their ancestry, over which they had no choice, and partly the result of their early education and environment, which also was not of their own selection. Therefore, by the time they are old enough to determine their actions for themselves, their habits and characters are to a large extent already formed.

There is too much of the presumption that all men have an equal chance in the battle against temptations, and too little acknowledgment of the part played by heredity and environment. True, we can overcome these by the exercise of our will, but such strong will, such tenaciousness to keep to one's resolution, is also due to our hereditary organisation and the stimulus of the environment. Each man has his breaking point. This breaking point varies in different people, and in the same person is different for different temptations; and if he is tempted in this direction beyond his strength he will fail.

We are all of us a compound of our inborn qualities and those that have been stamped, as it were, upon us by contact with the external world; and we have no right to judge in an offhand manner of the innate qualities of an offender without a very extensive knowledge of the upbringing and of the temptations, and influences to which he has been subjected. The healthy boy does not live who has not committed acts which would bring him within the pale of the law were he of age and caught in his mischief and the usual legal remedies dispensed to him. The child of good parentage may get the spanking, and his selfish disregard for the rights of others will eventually be replaced by altruism. The child who has no parents or too indulgent parents or vicious parents may end one day in gaol.

Among the internal dispositions, in themselves moral, but which may be used immorally, are: lust for wealth, desire for social supremacy, ambition, love of notoriety, and love of display. Among external causes which may weaken the moral character are: irregular family life, lack of proper training or a definite training in wrong-doing, mental irritations, disappointments and conflicts, a faulty attitude to life and society, bad companions and pernicious literature.

The young child, if morally neglected, manifests his animal propensities without restraint and grows selfish and self-indulgent. Not having learned to subordinate his propensities or instincts to social requirements, his natural trend is not altruistic. On the other hand, not all children are educable to the required standard. Some can be brought only to a certain degree of perfection, while others fall away when left to act by themselves. In other words, there are always some incapable of taking an artificial education of self-control. In this respect they resemble the tamed and trained animal, which can act contrary to his instincts, but soon relapses, if left alone; while some are not educable at all.

Some parents are too indulgent. They may fail to punish a child for his misdeeds, and the child may have defects which the parents fail to recognise or may even encourage. Such, for example, is the tendency to romancing. Their stories may have an element of real truth, but are embellished unduly by a too lively phantasy. I remember a delinquent girl with a remarkable gift of invention. On one occasion her mother had rebuked her for some misdeed and ordered her to go and pray to God to forgive her for the sin she had again committed. After a while the mother inquired of her daughter whether she had done as she was told. "Yes, Ma'," was the reply, "and God said, 'Don't mention it, Miss Brown!'"

Sometimes excessive authority on the part of the parents develops the rebel type, that type of child who is openly hostile to all authority and looks upon rules and regulations as only made to be broken. I have known a daughter fail at the same age as her mother, who had a past, and had taken the severest care to bring up her child virtuously. Just this abnormal restraint caused the girl to revolt, and on the first opportunity she ran away with a young man. There must be firm and wise direction of the growing life, but the weight of authority should be steadily diminished till it reaches the vanishing point as the young person ends his or her teens. We must have discipline from without at first, but we want to develop later on internal discipline and mastery over self. Strict discipline must be tempered by love. I have seen children, who lost their mothers, described as backward, when they simply lacked the influence of affection to induce them to learn.

The morals of humanity depend largely upon the training it gets at the mother's knee. The home and the maternal influence are the most powerful agents in repressing anti-social acts. Woman, as a rule, exercises a refining influence, antagonistic to the instinctive coarseness of man's nature. For her approbation he is inspired to noble deeds, and desirous of holding the respect of the community. For her, and for his children, he has that courage and ambition in the battle of life which, as a celibate, he might lack.

One of the chief causes of misconduct is lack of proper education. This may sound incredible, considering that the cases that come before the mental specialist belong nearly all to the wealthier classes of society. I had better explain, therefore, what I mean by lack of education. Of course, all children are trained to read, write, and calculate, and to acquire the special knowledge necessary for the pursuit for which the parents intend them. But their education finished, they discard all their books and read no more, have no interest outside sporting and theatrical gossip, and the murder and divorce cases reported in the daily newspaper. This total neglect of training to appreciate anything approaching intellectual enjoyment is one of the causes of so many seeking the lowest forms of sensual enjoyment, with all the demoralisation associated therewith. Their moral education extends only so far that they can conduct themselves as ladies and gentlemen in society, and does not include the inculcation of self-control, self-denial, and the habit of taking a healthy, kindly interest in everything and everybody. No wonder they are easily "bored" and seek for excitement, with all its consequences. If the whole personality had been harmoniously developed, such a condition would be impossible.

A large number of people, whose education has been wrongly conducted, lack the motives which would counteract selfish and immoral tendencies. They have no "worship" except Mammon; no "wonder," except that excited by the sight of a nude or semi-nude figure; their conjugal affection is mere sex-gratification; they have no time to develop family attachment, being always at their business, at their club, at their golf; they have no æsthetic sensibility, though they may boast of possessing an old master, whom they appreciate only for the sum they paid for the work; and they have no charity, no real interest in deserving cases or benevolent institutions. As a lady once replied to me: "Is it not enough if I write out the cheques?"

A large number of people commit acts of indiscretion, if not actual crime, through imprudence, an unfortunate fit of passion, poverty and sore need, or from other very pressing external circumstances. They have fallen once and may never fall again. But if, as is sometimes the case, they are completely disgraced by their first fall or punished unduly, they may get so disgusted with society that they continue their evil ways; or, even if not at all resentful, circumstances may be such afterwards, that they have no chance to rise again.

The moral and the immoral person may feel equally strong urgings, but the one chooses legal methods for his gratification, while the other takes the law into his own hands, regardless of social restraint. For example, theft by a person in necessity need by no means imply so vicious a temperament as that of a man who spends his life in getting the better of his less clever neighbours, and who enriches himself by the loss of others, as is done in many so-called legitimate ways.

Necessity has no such influence on women, as a rule, for a large proportion of them are protected from want by marriage, when the man will do the deed; and spinsters, if confronted with want or desirous to live in greater luxury than their circumstances warrant, take to an immoral life sooner than to actual crime.

As regards the most dangerous age, it is certainly the period of adolescence, for the individual is then receiving impulses which he has not yet the judgment to control. The rebellion against authority and the desire for many new experiences arise, which previously have not been even dreamed of. There may be exaltations and depressions and morbid imaginations, and peculiar fault-findings and dissatisfaction with home surroundings. Fortunately many of these peculiarities are temporary; but the troubles arising from the newly awakened sex-impulses may be lasting.

Susceptibility to suggestion is one of the most common factors of misconduct. It is not alone the mentally defective who are so highly suggestible; we are all suggestible in accordance with our most active propensities and dispositions. Even a person in the hypnotic state will refuse to perform any act which is contrary to his or her natural disposition. But both normal and hypnotised people will readily accept any notion for which their own nature has already prepared them. The morally sound will grow up normally even among criminal surroundings; but there are a vast number of individuals who are so organised, so little balanced, or with such strong propensities of their own, that outside influence may just give the stimulus to turn them to evil habits. It is these folks who have to be protected from association with dissolute or criminal people; it is these folks who are easily influenced by immoral and crime literature, whose restraint is easily reduced by the display counters of great stores; it is these folks who are susceptible to the suggestion imparted by the apparent safety and profit of a given form of vice and crime.

The most common cause of misconduct is, no doubt, mental defect. In Parkhurst Prison, among a daily average of over 750 convicts, "the number classified as weak-minded at the end of the year was 117, but in addition 34 other convicts were attached to parties of weak-minded for further mental observation." And "during the year 35 convicts were certified as insane and sent to asylums." If a person is so defective that he cannot earn his living, he will take more readily an immoral course, probably to robbery. The mental defect may not be very apparent while he is sheltered in his home. It may manifest itself only when he has to provide for himself and face the difficulties that meet him in the world. As a rule, work is drudgery to him, for he cannot learn. He may succeed for a long time before he is caught, for often he is cunning, though weak-minded. Cunningness is not a sign of intelligence. Even idiots can be very cunning. As a rule, however, the mental defect that is taken note of is of a more marked type, and amounts to actual mental weakness. To this class belong the foolish odds and ends of humanity, the people of no foresight. Some are given to trivial offences often repeated; for example, the theft of certain articles only. Others commit a number of apparently purposeless offences. Mentally defective girls become easy victims to sexual immorality.

Mere lack of intelligence is not a motive to crime. Even defectives have sometimes special abilities and know, in their particular sphere at least, how to guard themselves. They can be moral, if they have no strong instincts, though they are defectives. Mental inferiority—intellectual, emotional, or volitional—forces no one to steal or burgle.

In most cases the mental defect consists primarily in the incapacity of the individual to adapt himself to the requirements of society without external supervision or support. Ability to do this may be regarded as the essential quality of the normal mind, and it is by no means synonymous with ability to pass the psychological tests, which are now so commonly applied. In many of our schools, and in most American institutions for youthful delinquents, the ability of mental defectives is being tested. This is excellent, so long as we realise that these tests are measurements of general intelligence and not of special ability or of character. Even in the case of tests which are tests of character and most nearly approach social situations, there is still a great difference between passing them in a laboratory and under the stress and strain of real life. If a youth is asked how he would behave in certain circumstances, he may readily reply as he is expected to, but this would be no indication of his actual conduct. For the one is a theoretical question, appealing chiefly to his intelligence; the other is the result of certain emotions and impulses which the temptation arouses in him and which urge him towards certain acts. How strong the particular emotion or propensity may be at any given moment cannot be foretold. As Mr. Cyril Burt, the able psychologist of the London County Council, has said: "The defective child has not the necessary intelligence to perceive for himself, or to bear effectively in mind, that what tempts him is dishonest, and that dishonesty is wrong—base in itself, and bad policy in the long run." And this is true of most of our occasional evil-doers, whether they lapse into theft or some other crime.

The heredity of immoral tendencies and crime is simply through mental defect. It is not the evil-doing or criminality that is inherited, but the incapacity to acquire the higher and more complex associations required for good and social conduct. True, there is no criminal type. But since there is no definite knowledge of the "mental" functions of the brain—the few theories which have been advanced contradicting one another—and since there is no agreement whether one can tell the size and shape of the brain by the size and shape of the head, there is no information available as to what constitutes a good or a bad head, except that supplied by phrenology, which, in the opinion of our scientists, has been dead and buried long ago. What they have in their minds is the popular exposition by professional character readers, and not the scientific observations made by Gall in extreme cases. Since there is no other theory in existence, I have availed myself of a modified phrenological system based on the effects of circumscribed brain lesions (see *Encyclopædia Britannica*, article "Phrenology," by Professor Alexander MacAlister) whenever I have been consulted about mentally or morally deficient children, and that my diagnosis was correct is proved by their subsequent careers, of which in many cases I was able to keep a record, their trials and convictions being reported in the newspapers. The point I want to emphasise here is, that I have seen many children adopted by good people, and brought up with the utmost care, who have turned out bad in later years. They had abnormal types of head. And the moral I want to draw is that no child should be adopted without a strict medico-psychological examination.

Of course, not every degenerate is a criminal. Many of them are happy and innocent enough, but when they belong to the very poor and cannot get enough to eat or a place wherein to sleep, they may steal, beg, sleep out, or commit some other offence that brings them within the meshes of the law, and become criminal. They become criminals, not because they possess criminal minds, but because there is no place for them in our social and industrial life and their necessities cannot be supplied in any other way.

A recent annual report of the Prison Commissioners tells us of convicts, that "on an average they are two inches less in height and fourteen pounds less in weight than the average industrial population of similar ages; 28 per cent. of them suffer from some physical disease or deprivation," and "the highest proportion of re-convictions was amongst this class, being no less than 40 per cent." In a word, weakness, not wickedness, is the great cause of crime. But bodily weakness does not of necessity produce any tendency to moral failing. Only when it is the cause of mental dulling may there be moral lethargy and consequent establishment of anti-social habits. On the other hand, excess of physical vigour may give rise to certain forms of misconduct. There are some individuals, misplaced in an environment which does not call forth all their powers, whose very superabundance of animal spirits makes for immoral tendencies. The healthy, strong, and prematurely developed girl, for example, is often a source of anxiety to her parents. Frequently the main point is the lack of correlation between physical over-growth and childlike type of mental powers. But even in an adult, mentally normal, too great surplus of general or special energy under the conditions of town life may occasionally lead directly to anti-social conduct, especially fighting and bullying.

Degeneration of the arteries and malnutrition of the brain as affecting the instrument of the mind, often give rise to particular forms of misconduct, which will be described in their respective chapters. Under this heading come also poisons circulating in the blood, and the secretions of certain glands which have an influence on the functioning of the brain.

One cause of immorality and crime, which is almost totally neglected, and of which, as will be shown in later chapters, I have seen a large number of cases, is that of head-injury. I can give no statistics, but one or two criminologists who have made investigations in that direction claim to have found as many as 11 per cent. of the prisoners they had examined to have suffered injury to the head.

Finally, I should like to make a few remarks on the professional criminal, though he has not come under my special observation, except in the prisons I visited here and in foreign countries. Naturally, the cold-blooded assassin or poisoner, the professional burglar or housebreaker who does not always hesitate to take human life if he is interrupted, the person who commits clever and carefully calculated gigantic frauds—these people do not consult the medical psychologist. But it may be as well to point out some of the characteristics which distinguish the professional criminal from the types of wrong-doers so far described.

Crime, to the professional criminal, is an occupation, an employment, or a business taken up as the outcome of environment, education, training, and circumstances, and entered upon as a means of trying to make a living; at least with many, especially of the lower orders. In the higher classes, where circumstances are favourable and the training sound, it is frequently one member of the family only who goes wrong. Then the case is more likely to be pathological. The professional criminal is callous to reprobation, loves low pleasures and prefers easy gain to steady labour. Many possess average mental powers, and some of them a grasp of intelligence, a tenacity of purpose, and a strength of will in the plan and execution of crime which, had they applied their powers and industry to social ends in conformity with social rules, would have raised them to virtuous eminence. Professional crime may be the outcome of vicious passion which a low intelligence is powerless to guide and control; yet it may also denote a will served by an acute and entirely self-seeking intelligence, sagacious to devise and skilful to execute criminal enterprises. The want, then, is not intellectual; it is lack of that finest feeling of social responsibility which is known as moral sense. The professional criminal plans crime as the merchant plans business. He thinks dishonesty a paying game. He never has worked, and he does not want work. He prefers living by his wits. The regularity of life which work entails is more than he can bear. Punishment is no deterrent to him, for he looks to the chances of escape.

He may feel and dread the material consequences of crime, but his conscience is not strong enough to torture him for his guilt. Repentance is rare. Fear in him is a deterrent, but not a reformatory emotion. Therefore he relapses whenever there is any assurance of safety to himself. He takes his chance, and if he fails he blames himself only for carelessness in neglecting some point essential to his success in accomplishment or concealment.

Crime as a profession may be chosen because of its sporting nature, in preference to the more monotonous, tame, and toned-down humdrum life of good citizenship. The professional criminal is a natural gambler, who knows the ruling of the social law, and he accepts the challenge with the full power of his reasoning faculties. It is a gamble that is frequently successful; frequently enough to make it worth his enterprise. The world knows only of the failures; proclaims that crime seldom goes unpunished, that "murder will out," and the like; whereas the truth is, as many a criminal has occasion to know, that crime is often undetected, and when detected often goes unpunished, that murders are done which are not suspected, murders suspected which are not detected, and murders detected which are not always duly punished.

CHAPTER III

DRINK AND DRUG HABITS

THE ALCOHOLIC.

THE desire for food and drink is a primary instinct for the preservation of the individual. It arises from hunger and thirst, the satisfying of which gives us great sensory enjoyment. The abnormalities of the desire for food—such as voraciousness and gluttony on the one hand, and the insane refusal of food and the delusional fear of food on the other—need not detain us; nor the strange cravings of the appetite as witnessed sometimes in pregnant women. The impulse to eat, if gratified excessively or perversely, brings its own punishment; so does often a morbid desire for drink, but unfortunately not always. Man, unlike the animal, is not satisfied with plain water. He wants a stimulant, and it seems that ever since his existence on earth he was addicted to some kind of alcoholic beverage; not because of its taste, but because of the sensation it produces.

The man with a refined and normal nervous system, and the man with any real aspiration to succeed or excel, will abstain from everything that tends to blunt the higher mental functions and susceptibilities. If alcoholic drink disagrees with him, he will not take it; and there can be no doubt whatever that many people would be better without it. The great majority drink only with their meals, when alcohol, especially in the form of wine, may help the digestion; but most people indulge in it, not on that account, but merely from social custom and because they like it. If they drink between meals, it is either because they are thirsty and plain water is not always available or pure or tasty, and non-alcoholic drinks to many people are insipid; or else, because they are in convivial company, when it is sociable to drink a glass of wine or diluted spirit with your host. One of its effects is to relax inhibition, whereby it promotes freer social intercourse and mutual co-operation. It is not for nothing that dinners play so large a part in raising funds for charitable objects. A moderate amount of alcohol makes people more contented and cheerful.

But we are not concerned here with the minor causes that induce people to take alcohol, or with the question whether it is a food, a depressant or a stimulant, or with the problem whether the country would do well to go "dry." What we are concerned with is the deeper reasons for drinking which produce harmful effects and may lead a person to become a "drunkard" or "alcoholic." As a rule, where there is drinking to excess, there is a predisposition to do so. This predisposition is of a twofold nature. It may consist of an attraction towards alcohol, in consequence of which the habit is very quickly established; or of an intolerance of alcohol, in consequence of which small quantities suffice to produce brain disturbances.

Just as people differ in all other respects, so they differ in their disposition and susceptibility to the charm of alcohol. To most of us, alcohol has no temptation. There is no particular merit in that we do not drink, or drink only moderately; neither is there any restraint, but we simply have no desire for it. Most people could not get drunk if they tried. They are drink-proof, not because of any superior virtue, not because of any superiority of self-control, but because drink has for them no temptation. Others have such unpleasant sensations if they exceed a small quantity of alcohol that they are compelled to leave off long before they have taken enough to make them drunk. They remain sober without effort. The quantity needed to produce distaste varies much in different persons. The important difference is that, in some persons, satiety is produced before intoxication; and in others, intoxication is produced before satiety. Among those who are liable to become intoxicated before reaching the point of satiety, there are many who refuse to indulge further the desire for drink. Their self-respect and desire to retain the respect of others, or the knowledge that they will make beasts of themselves, gives them the power of self-control. Some succumb from time to time; others become habitual drunkards. The intolerance is greatest in persons who are predisposed to diseases of the nervous system, or whose nervous system is actually disordered, and those who exhibit mental instability.

It is natural that ne'er-do-weels, profligates, persons of lax morality, should take to drink; but it is not the drink that makes them so. Such persons, when once accustomed to alcohol, often experience an increasing sense of ill-being when deprived of it for any length of time, and their craving becomes uncontrollable. Not every one who drinks, even to excess, is an alcoholic; only those persons can be regarded as such who either continually or at certain periods suffer from a craving for alcohol. Intolerance of alcohol should always raise a suspicion of a latent pathological condition. Often the mental trouble is masked by alcoholic indulgence.

To no class of persons is intemperance more dangerous than to those inheriting an unstable nervous system. Speaking generally, the insane, the weak-minded, the epileptic, and those who have sustained grave head injuries, are susceptible in unwonted degree to the evil influence of alcohol. They are profoundly affected by an amount that would cause only a mild exhilaration in a more stable organisation. I have seen insane patients, in whom I could trace head injury, whose insanity dated from the day when they partook of alcohol, though not in excess of the dose they were accustomed to take before their injury.

Those who lack mental balance are usually more readily intoxicated, and every drink they take creates a morbid desire for more drink, overcomes the will, blunts the moral sensibilities, and makes everything subservient to its demands; until the habitual intoxicating cup thrusts itself perpetually upon their thoughts, gradually excluding all other ideas.

Where there is an inherently stable nervous system excessive drinking is liable to produce cirrhosis of the liver, and from the fact that liver disease is rare in alcoholic insanity—it is hardly ever found in asylums—we may deduce that most people will tolerate any amount of alcohol, up to extensive physical disease, without becoming insane; and that this only happens when there are other important factors present.

Among the contributory causes, especially in women, are early training and example, grief, worry, jealousy, loneliness, ennui from lack of occupation, mental depression, and free access to alcohol. Men take it for its power of lessening the feeling of fatigue and physical discomfort, and for the cheerfulness produced which makes them forget their troubles. Sometimes the habit has its origin in physical conditions and disappears with their treatment.

We are all influenced by social opinion which

regards drunkenness with disgust. Therefore, the more public drinking-places are made, the greater the restraining influence. People rarely get drunk in restaurants, and more commonly so in public-houses and saloon bars.

Drunkenness is commonest in those who drink for oblivion or stupefaction; less in those who drink for stimulation and excitement. Those who drink for stimulation are usually steady drinkers. Before they can attempt any mental or physical task they must have recourse to alcoholic stimulation. In them, a considerable quantity is required before intoxication is produced.

The person who takes to drink in order to forget his or her troubles and misfortunes must be already a weak character; for to obtain their end they must use increasing quantities of alcohol. Indulgence gives temporary relief; the experiment is repeated; the power of the will is still further sapped; the consciousness of the practice, the sense of degradation, is now added to the pre-existing misery; and the remnants of self-restraint and of self-respect are swept away in the current of a resistless stream. The patient then does not seek the pleasing sensation of intoxication. He drinks rather to escape from a state of sobriety which has become intolerable. Resolutions to break himself of the habit may be made, but the patient has lost the capacity to maintain a resolution.

Doubtless a few cases of alcoholism can be attributed

solely to force of example, but even in these we must consider the brain disposition of the person upon whom the example exerts its influence. In the cases I have seen where one of the parents was habitually addicted to drink, the children had a horror of it. Only where drink was the rule without drunkenness did the children also get accustomed to it.

Women differ from men in that they have no strong desire for alcohol. Many actually dislike it; but if they once take to it in any quantity, a craving is easily induced and they can no longer stop themselves. Some women who have acquired the taste for alcohol are so thoroughly ashamed of their bad habits that they drink secretly; until the habit becomes established, when certain symptoms appear which betray the chronic alcoholic. So insidiously does the habit commence and grow, so secretly is it practised and the habit formed, that it is some time before the dreadful knowledge forces itself upon their friends. The patient's striving to resist explains why her excesses occur periodically in a recurrent manner. After the excess is over, the woman is full of repentance, asks for forgiveness and vows never to do it again; but like the man, unless treated, all her good resolutions vanish at the first opportunity or the first occasion when she feels grieved or unhappy.

Alcohol impairs efficiency and diminishes staying power. The amount of output may perhaps be increased to a small extent for a time, but the increase soon falls off and is replaced by a diminution. The influence upon the psychical side is more profound. It leads immediately to a feeling of renewed vigour and increased strength; but here also the effect is transitory. The physical discomfort of fatigue is diminished by alcohol; that is why it is taken more often towards the end of the day, when a tired feeling has set in.

When alcohol is imbibed freely we have first of all slight excitement and a feeling of well-being, in which speech and gestures become more animated. There is at first a paralysis of the inhibitory apparatus, the loquacious stage, when the person becomes talkative, gay and lively. He thinks he is very funny and witty, when perhaps he is uttering the most commonplace remarks, or reiterating the most fatuous statements. The general expression becomes one of silly self-satisfaction, with a fatuous smile, which may be blended with a look of astonishment. The curb which fear of public opinion puts on the free expression of emotions is removed, whence the justification for the saying *in vino veritas*. He will insist upon shaking hands repeatedly, and is anxious to tell strangers his private affairs, especially grievances which he will exaggerate and to which he will keep alluding, suffering from a partial loss of memory. Later the ideas become crowded together and confused.

Whether in the stage of excitability the person

will tend towards joy, melancholy, or anger depends on his natural dispositions and the environment. But there is certainly a greater tendency to become argumentative and even pugnacious, and to become profane, obscene, abusive, threatening and maybe violent.

The exaggerated feeling of strength and well-being at the onset of the intoxication soon passes, and the movements become poorly controlled, the gait becomes staggering and the speech thick. So long as the person is seated he may speak and discuss subjects quite distinctly and rationally; yet when he attempts to walk, he may not be able to take one step—in fact, may not be able to stand. On the other hand, he may be able to walk quite steadily, yet be unable to articulate one word. This particular stage of drunkenness often leads to considerable difficulty in police-court cases. For the person in this condition has lost control of the muscles of locomotion, but has control of the muscles in connection with speech, and, having steadied himself against the counter, he can speak coherently and quite distinctly. The policeman, having seen the staggering gait, swears that the man was drunk; the bar-attendant, having heard the clear speech, declares the man was sober, otherwise he would not have supplied him.

The excitement commonly associated with drunkenness is not the direct effect of alcohol, but of its dulling action upon the highest powers of the brain, judgment, and self-criticism. This releases the lower faculties, the propensities, from control, which then respond to any slight stimulus. As drinking continues, self-control is progressively weakened until suspended. Not only are the lower faculties released, but sometimes latent or carefully concealed traits of character and suppressed desires of insufficient intensity to invade the field of sober consciousness come to the surface and assert themselves when artificially freed from superior control.

Acute alcoholism generally follows excessive drinking in otherwise normal persons, but what may be excess to one person need not be so to the other. Persons suffering from shock, distress, physical diseases, accidents, or any brain defect, temporary or permanent, and lastly persons not accustomed to alcohol, may feel the effects of its intoxication after very small quantities, which would have no effect at all on the habitual drinker. Acute alcoholism generally develops suddenly. Its chief mental characteristics are terror, mental distress, and confusion of ideas. Repugnant visual hallucinations are frequent, and the patient may smell or taste poisons. Chief amongst the physical signs is a fine muscular tremor, most marked when the attention is distracted.

I had one patient, a lady, who drank very heavily all her life; her husband, too, was a heavy drinker. She had weaned herself, but two years later she still had hallucinations, seeing creepy things that used to disturb her formerly in her alcoholic delirium.

Chronic alcoholism shows itself in gradual and progressive mental deterioration and in certain physical changes. The ordinary public-house drunkard is of the noisy, hilarious type. The habitué of the West-End club is talkative to the various members, cantankerous, irritable, and infirm of purpose, liable to be quarrelsome if contradicted or crossed in any way. The chronic alcoholic gradually undergoes a change in character. He becomes untruthful, loses his finer sense of honour ; he, little by little, grows lax about things concerning which he was formerly most particular. He becomes indifferent to his own interests and regardless of the feelings or prosperity of his relatives and family. He sees those depending on him suffering from want and shame, yet pursues his downward course seemingly indifferent to their needs or their entreaties. Sometimes he falls so low that he will pawn or sell his wife's property that he may procure money to buy more drink. Another striking feature is an unreasonable irritability, which frequently leads to outbursts of passion of a blindly impulsive character, of which his family or his associates are often the victims. Wife-beating, inhuman treatment of children, attacks upon associates on the slightest provocation, are of daily occurrence during the stage of inebriety.

Alcohol inflames the emotions and excites the sexual passion, and many a young person under its influence—perhaps for the first time—contracts venereal disease; and this fact is of great importance in the consideration of the effects of alcohol in relation to the infertility of intemperate women. Drunkenness and immorality often go together, especially in women. Even when there is no intellectual decay, there is a deterioration in the moral sphere. Cunning and untruthfulness are leading characteristics and most marked in the female dipsomaniac. Women who, up to the time of contracting the alcoholic habit, were regarded as uniformly truthful and honest in every relation of life, now totally disregard the good opinion of their friends. There is no strategy, no humiliation, no sacrifice too great for the purpose of obtaining the, to them, necessary stimulant.

Delusions referring to the sexual functions are not uncommon. Consequently jealousy and suspicion of infidelity, of the husband by the wife and the wife by the husband, frequently occur, and may end in murderous assaults. It must be, however, remembered that there is sometimes a basis of truth in these accusations. Also not infrequently a woman takes to drink because of the cruelty or infidelity of the husband; and the converse is also true.

I have no doubt that many people drink to make them sexually more excitable, and sometimes they overstep the mark and get drunk. This would explain why women whose husbands are unfaithful so frequently take to drink, especially when they are approaching the climacteric.

Chronic alcoholism may lead to crimes of acquisitiveness and lust, violence and homicide, but the alcoholic is not primarily a criminal; just as the criminal may drink as an incident in his life of crime but is not primarily an inebriate. Suicide is not uncommon in consequence of mental depression, and insanity is frequent. In all the forms of alcoholic insanity there is an undue suspicion against the environment, and if delusions are present they tend to be of a persecutory nature.

For the true inebriates there is no temperance question; there is only an absolute need for total abstinence. Nothing can ever make intoxicating substances safe for inebriates. They are without the safeguards of normal men, and to them intoxicating substances are, and always must be, poisons. They are affected by the alcoholic poison both quickly and deeply, as is shown by the rapid general deterioration which they manifest when once they begin to drink, and by their inability to regulate their drinking in a way that normal persons can do.

When the weaning from the alcohol habit has been effected, not by a scientific psychotherapy, i.e. by re-education of character and restoration of the normal working of the mind, but by compulsion, this compulsion is very apt to excite a latent hostility which remains as a subconscious fixed idea to revive at some moment of weakness under the guise of a return of craving. This is undoubtedly the reason why restraint fails to produce a lasting cure in many cases of alcoholic addiction, and it shows the extreme importance of accurate psychological study in dealing with persons of this sort. In each case we have an individual problem to face with its own particular life-history, which must be probed and analysed to unearth the sources of the mental current which has induced drink as a refuge. Moreover, mental conflicts must be removed.

Psychotherapy is the most important treatment. There are different methods, as described in Chapter XII of this work; but a sound psychotherapist will not confine himself to any single one. No two cases are alike, for no two characters are precisely alike nor are the causes the same in each case; therefore they cannot be successfully treated by any stereotyped plan. In each case we have an individual problem to face with its own particular life-history and its own particular mental conflicts, which must be probed and analysed to unearth the sources of the mental unrest which has induced drinking as a refuge. Certain conditions must be produced, in which the patient can be made to realise vividly the danger to himself and others certain to accrue from his drinking habits; he must be made to see the necessity for complete abstention from alcohol in any form, for though others may be able to take it in moderation, he is not built like others; and he must be made to feel that his achieving success will depend to a large extent on his perseverance in steady work and regular habits.

Further, let me emphasise that psychotherapy alone is incomplete without physical measures. All the relapses are due to this neglect. Not only does the patient during the treatment require medicinal assistance to make him feel comfortable, but he wants building up afterwards to enable him to carry out his will and resolutions. Therefore the curative measures employed must be directed to bring about improvement in the general health of the patient and to increase his bodily and nervous strength.

Freud and his followers give a singular explanation of the addiction to alcohol, and claim to achieve its cure by the method of psychoanalysis. According to the Freudian doctrine, alcoholics have a large homosexual complex. Homosexuality is an intolerable idea, conflicts with conscious trends of thought, and is therefore repressed. Whenever it subsequently escapes the repression, it is bound to give rise to intrapsychic conflict. This is too much for the individual to bear, and he therefore seeks comfort in alcohol. The manner in which this achieves its object varies from patient to patient, and it can only be revealed by psychoanalysis. I have already shown that there are many factors that induce people to drink to excess, and that we must discover the cause by a searching analysis of the mental organisation and history of the patient. Whatever be the treatment adopted, the lowered bodily health and nervous energy must be attended to. But the chief reason why treatment by psychoanalysis by the strictly orthodox method is impractical is, that few patients can spare the time and money to visit the specialist "daily for at least four months," the minimum period claimed by psychoanalysts to achieve a cure. Many of my patients have been broken of the habit within fourteen days and then attended once a week, and then once a month, until all likelihood of a relapse had disappeared.

One word more about the female inebriate. Women as a rule have no desire for alcohol. Most of them would go without it all their lives if they were not induced by men, or acquired the habit from women older than themselves. The first dose is often taken to bring on, or ease the discomforts of, the period.

Of most women it may be said that they drink alcohol just as they smoke tobacco, because they see men do it. Few women take drink to excess, unless there be some moral weakness. Indulgence in alcoholics is the Open Sesame to many a woman's virtue. Intoxicants are dangerous enough to men; to women they are positively disastrous. The virtue of the woman with the drink habit is always in danger. What might safely be considered moderate indulgence in men is decidedly immoderate in women. The woman with an uncontrollable appetite for liquor will sell her person for the purpose of securing money with which to purchase the desired stimulant.

It has been freely stated that when a woman becomes a drunkard she may be regarded as hopeless; in fact, that her reformation is practically impossible. Such expressions of opinion are entirely erroneous and do harm by instilling into the minds of the inebriate women the hopelessness of struggling against their failing. I have had a large number of women in private care, secret drinkers as well as women whose vocation exposed them to the temptation of drink, and can vouch that quite a number of them have become teetotalers and remained such. If a patient is willing to be treated, there is as a rule no difficulty in curing her. Only the women without sober intervals, and who have already lost all sense of shame and responsibility, are difficult to treat in private care. For them, the only hope is the "inebriate home."

The Drug Taker.

The quest for the temporary relief and artificial pleasure that can be derived from drug intoxication drives a good many people to its use. Sometimes certain drugs are resorted to, in the first instance, to get rid, for a time at least, of the pain, discomfort and wretchedness; that is, for the transient soothing effects. Sometimes drugs are taken directly for their stimulating effects, to rouse mental activity and to cope more readily with the artificial pleasures of social life. But the happiness is short, the mental energy transient, the relief is brief, and the destructive effects of drugs upon the mind and body are a high price to pay for soothing self-gratification. To many people, especially brain workers, even the ordinary tasks of daily life produce a sense of exhaustion, which is temporarily relieved either by a narcotic which dulls the highest perceptive powers or by a stimulant which rouses the over-fatigued brain to additional effort. Some find the one method, some the other, the more effective. The drug taker feels braced up and he resorts to it again and again on the most flimsy pretext, until the day comes when the drug habit, with all its sinister consequences, has obtained the mastery over him. Prolonged indulgence often fails to give pleasurable sensations. Still the drug taker must go on in order to avert the crisis of withdrawal. A stopping of the habitual drug produces the severe symptom complex of the deprivation which we know as "craving," and which leads to a larger dose of the drug by which the symptoms are quickly relieved. The symptoms on the withdrawal without medical aid are so severe—insomnia, uncontrollable restlessness, maniacal mental condition, and sometimes suicidal tendency—that the victim is overcome by fear of them and is led deeper and deeper into the power of the drug, until all interest in life beyond that of satisfying his craving is gone, and to do this successfully he counts the world well lost.

Propinquity to intoxicating drugs or sedatives, a knowledge of their use and opportunities for their indulgence, are causes for addiction; consequently doctors and nurses form a considerable number of the victims. Amongst lay people, the careless transfer of a hypodermic syringe for injecting morphine to obtain relief from pain is often the starting point in a downward career of drug taking. Those who help themselves overlook the fact that the symptoms for which they seek relief may really be the signs of real mental or physical trouble, and that the drug taken often masks the symptoms of an underlying and undiagnosed disease.

Normal persons rarely become drug habitués. Most of the devotees I have seen were highly strung, over-sensitive, and nervous persons, quick in perception, acute in sensibility, lacking in balance and in backbone, eager to escape from the realities of life. The person who indulges in the drug habit to the detriment of himself and of those dependent on him, whose affairs are being neglected, whose health is being ruined, whose family through his indulgence is suffering from the deprivation of those necessaries to which they are entitled—such a person is on the border-line of insanity. Whatever peculiar characteristic of mind or accidental incident may determine the formation of the habit, when once it is formed the patient has a real disease, and he can only exist free from great physical and mental pain when he is under the influence of the drug to which he is addicted. The drug-taking habit is a secret one, as a rule. It commences as a vice, but the developed craving becomes a disease.

MORPHINE is taken for its quieting effect, which is very different from the stimulation of alcohol or cocaine. The two main classes of users of morphine are neuropathic individuals of good mental endowment, who sometimes regulate so well the use of the drug that they can go many years without a vast amount of bad effect ensuing; and, secondly, prostitutes and social failures who desire to deaden their sensibilities and appreciation of distressing circumstances.

When morphine is taken, the highest mental powers are the first to disappear: the appreciation of right and wrong, the fine regard for others, and the feeling of self-respect are diminished. The appeal of the home, of dependents, of the wife, or of children, cease to have force. There is indifference to distress, and the feeling of shame is gone. Lying and deceit become second nature. There is progressive deterioration of the mind.

Sometimes opium, of which morphine is a derivative, is eaten. I remember a schoolmaster, addicted to the habit, being arrested and detained as a "wandering lunatic." I discovered afterwards he had learned the practice from natives while overseas.

Sometimes the same patient goes from one drug

to another; from morphine to cocaine and alcohol, with a view of curing himself, but he still fails.

COCAINE acts differently from morphine. It fascinates by the rapidity with which it relieves exhaustion and dispels gloom, and by a delightful sense of mental and physical vigour. It first powerfully stimulates the brain, causing mental excitement and restlessness. The flagging nerve-cells are whipped into activity, and lassitude and fatigue pass. But this is accompanied by clouding of associations, and a marked depression of the central nervous system always succeeds the stage of excitement. At first sensuous feelings are aroused, to the extent of destroying all feelings of refinement, especially in women; while men soon find that their virility is completely extinguished. Consequently wives are distrusted and accused of infidelity. The patient frequently becomes impulsive and violent, may wilfully destroy valuable property by reason of some fantastic delusion, and may murderously attack his supposed persecutors or commit suicide in order to escape them. Altogether, the things that matter in life are no longer seen in their true perspective, duties are neglected, obligations repudiated, and the man becomes a mental wreck.

It is only the repentant sinner who visits the consulting-room and voluntarily seeks for help to overcome the disastrous effects following upon the indiscriminate use of strong drugs. When once a habit is formed it becomes all but impossible for the person addicted to drugs to renounce it without medical assistance, for the craving is stronger than the controlling powers and most patients are afraid of the suffering entailed while they attempt weaning themselves. Therefore, whatever treatment a doctor adopts, he must be able to guarantee painlessness.

It is said that the drug must be withdrawn gradually to avoid delirium and delusions; that sudden and absolute withdrawal would cause untold suffering. I am absolutely against this opinion. Only at the outset of my career have I seen a case suffering mental trouble from the complete withdrawal. I then learned my lesson, and am able to make the abstention easy. When the patient finds that complete withdrawal causes not even discomfort, the effect on him mentally is a joy to witness, and it makes the subsequent treatment easy. If one withdraws the drug slowly, the patient may go on quite well, till the minimum dose is reached, and then there will be the same amount of trouble, as if the whole dose had been stopped at once. All depends upon whether a physician trusts entirely to psychotherapy, or whether he realises that he must adopt medicinal and hygienic measures for strengthening the body and nervous system of the patient before attempting anything else. There is in all drug takers an unstable nervous equilibrium which must be treated. Psychotherapy alone will not cure the chronic drug taker His physique, and especially his cerebral tissues, are soaked with the poison and their functions undermined.

On the other hand, physical measures and medicinal substitutes alone will fail to bring about a cure. They must be seconded by influences that act on the patient's mentality. The best instincts have to be discovered and engaged, and as there is some element of good in every item of humanity, that element must be discovered and drawn out. As in all psychotherapy, the history and all the circumstances in the mental life of the patients must be gone into and the patient's character re-educated. Most important of all, he must be taught self-control. Restraint by others cannot achieve the same result as the patient's own resolution, strengthened by the acquisition of new habits, to have nothing more to do with narcotics. The patient, when discharged, gets instructions to continue home-treatment, and reports himself from time to time.

CHAPTER IV

AGGRESSIVENESS, ILL-TEMPER, AND VIOLENCE

ANOTHER propensity connected with the instinct of self-preservation is the *combative propensity*, which is really a complex tendency, being required for aggression as well as for self-defence. Since most animals live on other animals, i.e. on moving things, every creature must be able to stop, destroy and kill in order to obtain food. That is the necessary condition for their existence, which can only be satisfied by an adequate expression of aggressiveness. And since every animal is thus liable to be killed and devoured by others, it must be alive to, and able to remove, the dangers by which it is surrounded, and must be capable of inflicting injury on its foes in self-defence, i.e. it must possess a propensity to resent.

Both beast and man must be able to appease their hunger. The hungry beast is wont to be savage, and so too is sometimes the hungry man. Man, in addition, must be able, not only to defend himself, his family and property, but he must be able to repel all kinds of aggression, and must therefore be in a position to assail. He cannot always wait till he is attacked. Man has so much modified his animal instincts that it comes to him as a shock to be told that he has a propensity to fight and destroy. We must go to primitive man, when nature was still " red in tooth and claw " and the law of life was to kill or be killed. If man now fights with machine guns and tanks, instead of his nails and teeth, those enemies that would deprive him of his means of existence, it is the same primitive instinct which still actuates his mind. Human nature has not changed. The animal fights from impulse without any thought of the pain it inflicts. Man is often mindful of the pain he can cause ; he is artfully cruel, and " brutal " is not the word for it. Man must kill animals for food, and he kills sometimes for the mere sake of killing as in hunting, or in destroying the enemy as in war. Killing the opponent in a duel was legal at one time. Disputes are still settled by a fight amongst the uncultured classes ; and if it ends in death of one of the parties, the verdict may be manslaughter or murder. Killing is still legitimate in self-defence.

In individual civilised human beings the combative propensity manifests itself in a refined manner. Whereas primitive man resembled the animal in having to enter into combat and destroy to obtain the food necessary for life, in our own day this propensity is greatly modified and altered, because, as I have already mentioned, our great civil organisation has made money, by reason of its purchasing power, the chief protector of life. In course of time, civilisation has diminished the necessity of physical aggression and defence, and it is no longer necessary for man to kill his personal enemies by way of punishment. He has devised means of getting redress through the administration of justice. The instinct still exists but finds an outlet in friendly rivalry, games and sport.

The combative instinct in a person of small intellect leads to easy provocation, ready quarrelling, the kindling of strife, and sometimes noisy arguing, abusive language, and to unpremeditated—and to a lesser extent designed—violence. Combativeness with little caution leads to foolhardiness. When it is too strong, we get the born bully and the man who loves a fight for its own sake. Excessive indulgence in alcohol stimulates it; and even in those in whom it is ordinarily deficient the propensity may be roused by the severity of the combined injury and insult. There is no father who does not feel he would shoot the seducer of his daughter on the spot.

The propensity of resentment is accompanied and aroused by a special emotion—that of irascibility or *anger*. This emotion is necessary in order to stimulate the physical energy and give the animal strength for fight. When a man is angry, the spontaneous impulse is to inflict injury on the originating cause of the emotion awakened. Sometimes he destroys innocent objects to give vent to his anger.

Moralists weary not in their righteous denunciations of anger, but they might bring things to a sorry pass if they succeeded in abolishing it. Anger has its social justification, as it has its physiological basis, in the roused energies of the organism reacting against an impression hostile to its self-preservation and self-expansion; and its kindling in that case is self-assertive evidence of vital vigour in mind. Its discharge being natural and useful, the whole question of its wisdom or folly, of its benefit or hurt to the individual and society, is a question of degree and rule, of its wise dispersion and guidance, of the maintenance of the just mean. A mind insensible to anger would be nerveless and impotent, as a society in which everybody was meek and placid would be unprogressive, stagnant, and liable to corrupt. The right is the trite rule of nothing in excess; for a society in which everybody was self-assertive, aggressive, and revengeful must needs issue in tumult and disruption; while faithful observance of the rule to turn one cheek after the other to the smiter until he tired of smiting could not fail to put good men at the mercy of knaves and to strangle honesty in a wild growth of knavery.

Indulgence in feelings of anger and vindictiveness tends to make those subject thereto more and more habitually prone to outbreaks of passion. Frequent anger, commonly called *temper*, is unfavourable to sound judgment and unbiased opinion. Anger may be rational, but its highest pitch—rage—is brief madness; for the main characteristic of madness is loss of self-control, and this is exactly what happens to people in a passion. The instinctive fury, the violent and destructive mania of some madmen, is not different; it is only the same mental power acting in excess. Children show anger in primitive, unmasked fashion, by biting, scratching, howling, kicking, and smashing everything within reach. Disciplined persons often do the same. Owing to the advance of intellect, rage is no longer necessary for the overcoming of one's enemy; we can do much better by circumspect and deliberate skill.

I have seen both boys and girls addicted to violent rage without or on very slight provocation, who would destroy anything they could lay their hands on and be a positive danger to their playmates, making ferocious attacks on them with any instrument available. I have found that in very young children the cause is often to be found in premature and excessive feeding on animal food. On regular dieting and proper hygiene the natural disposition of the child was soon restored. But of course there are sometimes other causes, with which we shall deal presently.

Different individuals, owing to their native temperament, bodily health, and moral education, vary remarkably in their propensity to anger, as also in the pertinacity with which they cherish this passion. In some it is sudden and transient; while in others, though perhaps less hasty, it assumes a more deep and lasting character, settling into that malignant feeling called *revenge*. Anger is sudden and impulsive resentment, in which the hostile reaction against the cause of pain is unrestrained by deliberation; while revenge is deliberate and controlled resentment, retrospective, inflicting punishment for past injury. It is most marked in the savage, who has to avenge all wrongs offered to himself, his relations, his tribe. Revenge to him is a duty and a right.

Revenge within limits is one of the most naturally expressed emotional reactions, but it may follow upon anger as an obsessional phenomenon, and be as much a sign of the lack of self-control as anger itself is. The desire for revenge plays a considerable part in the production of criminal deeds of violence.

Bacon called revenge a kind of wild justice which the law ought to weed out, since it putteth the law out of office, and moralists are wont to denounce it as sinful. Nevertheless it has its good use in the social economy, which without it would hardly run so smooth a course. The fear of a person's revenge works directly and effectually to protect him from injury, and thus acts indirectly, yet largely and widely, to check wrong-doing in a community; indeed, like many small vices and virtues, the humble workings of which philosophy is too lofty to notice, such fear operates more powerfully and generally as a preventive force in the conduct of life than the exalted precepts of morality. An act of revenge is no real benefit to the doer, sweet though it be at first, since it rouses retaliatory passion and detrimental hostility, but it makes for the welfare of the social body; the private vice becomes in a measure a public virtue; the avenger, like the angry bee, sacrifices his private interest to the larger interests of the community. It is not the whole truth to say that revenge puts the law out of office; for it works deeply and widely to execute a humble and effective kind of social justice which the law cannot condescend to and lofty moral precepts hardly touch.

Vindictiveness is not called into play until some measurable injury is received; while pugnacity prompts to aggression on a minimum of provocation, that may not be appreciable except to the pugnacious person. Both, pugnacity and vindictiveness, are proper qualities in the fight with the bully and the dishonest, helping the survival of individuals and families. Even a reputation for these qualities is a protection against aggression. Valuable, however, as they are to the individual, as defences against aggression, yet, as contributing to strife and turbulence within the community, they are anti-social qualities, and no community can thrive unless it keeps them in check. The pugnacious person, when he has a grievance against some one, is often too exasperated to wait for the slow course of the law; or, maybe, his grievance is one of which the law does not take cognisance. Actual personal assaults may lead to manslaughter.

Hate often precedes and succeeds anger. The object of anger is particularly apt to be the object of hate. What anger accomplishes by a volcanic outburst, hate accomplishes in a slower, but surer and subtler way.

Envy is hate combined with a certain very compound concept. It is aroused by the superiority of some individual to ourselves, which we regard as a sort of hindrance or injury, against which consequently we feel resentment. If we make attempts to bring down its object to a lower level, to compass the ill of its victim, this is malice.

Jealousy, too, is a very complex compound of love, fear, suspicion, and often hate. In some it provokes sulks, in others fury, in others tears, in others revenge. Like hate, it depresses vitality and keeps the body in a peculiar explosive condition, so that violent paroxysms of anger suddenly burst forth at a touch. Jealousy is a species of envy, but the latter invariably is attached to real or supposed superiority, while jealousy attaches to equality, or even lower, and has therefore a wider signification.

Murder may be committed for gain, or for lust, or for revenge, or to secure the safety of the murderer, or unintentionally, in the course of committing some other felony, or to escape from some unhappy marriage, or for the good of the victim, or from some other motive. Medical psychologists are not concerned with deliberate murders, for gain or other object, but principally with murders that are committed under some form of excitement, emotional, alcoholic, or other, or follow delusional disorder Whether due to passion, alcohol, or delusion, there is bound to be a certain degree of mental instability. If the murderer were not mentally unstable, he would not be passionate or addicted to alcohol, nor would alcohol or passion have that effect upon him. The killing of a man in passion may be done by one who would be incapable of settling an old grudge by taking a mean advantage of an enemy. Chronic alcoholics are subject to persecutory hallucinations and delusions, and may turn on their supposed enemies and attempt to kill them. Wife-beating, inhuman treatment of children, attacks upon associates as the effect of blind passion, are common. Alcoholism and jealousy combined may cause wife murder. One of the most powerful predisposing factors is the knowledge of the possession of a weapon in all these cases. It acts as if by suggestion. Such individuals should never carry or handle a deadly weapon.

Assaults on a person, with or without intent to kill, are made in acute mania. There need be no delusion whatever; the crime is simply the outcome of ungovernable passion. In a court of law one would have to prove other symptoms of this mental disease. A person suffering from melancholia may kill his wife and children, again without delusion, only because of his abject depression and misery; or from a delusion of hearing voices which recommend or command him to do so. The paranoiac kills a stranger, mistaking him for his long-sought enemy. The murder is done openly, and he justifies it. These patients often object to the defence of insanity on their behalf. They do not like to be called insane, even if they risk their lives when on trial for murder.

Epileptics are prone to irritability and impulsiveness, which may exist in every degree, from the mere excess of irritable temper and irrational conduct to the most dangerous homicidal impulse and acts. The epileptic who is subject to strong convulsions is less liable to post-epileptic automatism with dangerous impulses (though I have been once ferociously attacked by a patient who had a severe fit in my consulting room) than the cases of minor epilepsy, which suffer from temporary loss of consciousness without convulsions. Sometimes there is neither convulsion nor loss of consciousness, but only fits of clouded consciousness—so-called masked epilepsy, in which the patient may conduct himself strangely. When the strange act is of an innocent nature, as getting into a bath fully dressed, or when the act is dangerous only to the epileptic himself, the peculiar mental condition is readily admitted; but if the patient kills his sweetheart without adequate reason, the law is not willing to acknowledge his lack of mental balance, but orders him to be hanged.

Personally, I admit masked epilepsy only where there is an epileptic family history or the patient has had major or minor fits before. I have published (in other books of mine) several cases of men suffering from undoubted epilepsy who were declared guilty of murder and subsequently hanged.

Malicious damage to property, especially setting on fire, is common among feeble-minded people. But there are manifold reasons for arson, and many types of individuals may be implicated. Under the conditions of modern insurance arson may be engaged in for profit, and even, in conspiracy, as a business. It also has long been practised as one of the easiest methods of revenge. On occasion it offers a chance of enjoyable excitement. Thus the word "pyromania," applied to fire-setting, as such, with its connotation of mental aberration, is often unwarrantably employed.

There are two kinds of anger: that of the asthenic person, where the tone of nervous system is lowered, and that of the full-blooded, plethoric, and "hypersthenic" person, who suffers from an accumulation of energy, the excess of which may discharge itself regularly as if by an explosion, but always remains in a state of tension. It is the latter type that is most liable to brute passion and all those outbursts which may bring him in conflict with his surroundings and sometimes with public order and the law.

The exhausted, fatigued man is *irritable*; the hot-headed, overcharged man is *irascible*. Needless to say the two types require different treatment: the asthenic, tonic treatment; the hypersthenic, sedative treatment. In the latter, anger and violent passion increase the congestion of the brain. Therefore everything that can cause increased flow of blood to the head is liable to produce excitement and loss of control; and methods and remedies which reduce the congestion often will bring the person so afflicted speedily round to his normal condition. I have often been called to patients suffering from an attack of acute mania while staying in their own homes, and found them engaged in smashing furniture and threatening the life of anyone approaching them. I have never experienced any difficulty in getting these patients quiet within a short time, though I had neither strait-jacket nor attendants to assist me.

For the reason stated, arterio-sclerosis, which causes an increase in blood-pressure, renders persons affected with it highly irritable and quick-tempered. The mere questioning of a patient of this kind, whether he was subject to fits of anger, made him fly up, and reply sharply: "Angry, angry, never!" Then, seeing he had betrayed himself, he continued in a slower and milder tone of voice: "But you should see me play with my children." No doubt his natural temperament was amiable, but the condition of his cerebral arteries caused him to resent readily even innocent remarks.

Boys and younger men, charged with a superfluity

of energy for which they get no outlet, as when confined to the house or office and getting insufficient exercise, are liable to have outbursts of temper, in which they may hit their companions and destroy objects, and plan mischief of some kind, and tease and bully their companions. Regular, useful, physical employment, hard manual labour, especially in the open, I have found most effective in restoring good conduct, even without any other treatment. These observations will show the reader that the emotions can be modified by physical measures, and that the mind enslaved by evil habits may be led to contract good ones by regulating the nervous energy.

In my recent work *In Search of the Soul* I have given a collection of cases in which head injury of the lower temporal region—and inflammation and tumours of that area—were followed by uncontrollable impulses of violence and a number of them by murderous assaults. Sometimes epilepsy followed the injury, and both the fits and the violent disposition were cured by removal of the irritant, whether depressing splinter of bone, accumulation of cerebro-spinal fluid, localised hæmorrhage, or new growth. Some of these cases were shown to be due to bullet wounds, and recovered, though treated as late as seven years after the injury.

Owing to the proximity of this region to the internal portion of the ear, affections of that organ may cause irritation of the adjacent brain area, and sometimes actual extension of the inflammation. Again, I have shown in a number of cases that fits of temper, destructive mania, and homicidal impulses, especially in children, may be due to that cause, and when the ear trouble was attended to, the mental symptoms disappeared.

CHAPTER V

MORBID SUSPICION, CUNNING, AND DECEITFULNESS

ANIMALS had to protect themselves against their numerous enemies to avoid destruction, and developed a tendency to concealment, which was also found useful in approaching their own prey, and a feeling of suspicion. Suspicion is a protective propensity and hence a necessary quality. To hide is as instinctive as to run away. Hiding is protective because it falsely suggests to the adversary that there is nothing for him to attack. It is the beginning of deceit. An animal cannot always protect itself by open force, and it must make up in cunning what it lacks in strength and courage. Hence it conceals itself or its intentions. Thus wild animals make use of innumerable arts for procuring food and escaping from their enemies. The hunter studies the habits of the animals he pursues, that he may lay his snares and shape his proceedings accordingly; so it is in human life. Those who are secretive and close in what regards themselves are vigilant in watching others with intent to discover, if they can, their sentiments and purposes. Cunning can outwit muscular strength, and tends to develop the intellect in one particular direction.

A person under the dominion of this propensity can conceal his own thoughts successfully and take a great interest in the concealed thoughts of others. This is the Sherlock Holmes type. Even small things, slight omissions, and the smallest peculiarities of man have their lessons for him, raise a suspicion, and are traced to their true source. To the guileless man such things generally go unnoticed. The mind of the secretive man has a familiarity with all underground channels of thought. He knows by instinct what the next move of the rogue is likely to be, and can trip him up. Consequently the saying, "Set a thief to catch a thief." The criminal who is deceitful prefers forgery, embezzlement, and fraud to theft, and will use poison rather than direct assault to kill a person.

Some men are by nature secretive, prone to duplicity, hypocrisy, and cunning, while others are frank and open. A certain endowment of this power is essential. People who give utterance to every thought and feeling which arises in their minds, and confide their private affairs in a reckless fashion, appear to be both foolish and a nuisance. A man but moderately endowed with this power may nevertheless keep his own counsel, if he is possessed of caution and good judgment. Such a man may be frank and overflowing with his friends, but he will save himself with strangers by his caution. The man who has a fair share of this power trusts little without good cause, takes little for granted, and consequently is seldom hoodwinked; whereas the frank man is liable to think others equally frank and truthful, and is easily deceived.

A suspicious person—as, for instance, a jealous man—may reason quite correctly, but he will misinterpret actual occurrences in accordance with the state of his feeling. In such cases it is not the reasoning that is wrong, but the premises that are ill-founded, actual occurrences being misinterpreted owing to the perverted emotional state. If the premises are conceded, then is the conclusion perfectly correct.

Suspicion renders people secretive; they penetrate the thoughts of others and try to conceal their own. They are rarely indiscreet, and are generally able to restrain the outward manifestation of their feelings. Secretiveness with little conscientiousness gives a cunning, deceitful disposition. A secretive, but social, person may sometimes communicate his feelings freely to his nearest friends, yet will seldom do so and will exercise more attachment than he expresses. Secretiveness in a person very acquisitive and not conscientious leads to the practice of tricks of trade.

With little suspicion, a person is generally frank, candid, cordial in disposition and intercourse with men, has few secrets of his own which he wishes to keep, and cares little about learning the secrets of others. He may disclose his faults as freely as his virtues. Combined with large caution, he may manifest great care and deliberation in laying plans, but be imprudent in the manner of execution. The unsuspecting person is sometimes too frank with strangers and may disclose his innermost thoughts to chance acquaintances.

If himself an honourable man, he will be inclined to fall into the mistake of thinking that others are actuated by the same moral feelings as himself. Such men will be led into many pitfalls by the wily and the designing.

The natural tendency of the man possessed of too much secretiveness is to shrink unreasonably from other eyes seeing into his mind and his pursuits. Metaphorically speaking, he hides himself away, and conceals the true emotions of his mind. At the same time he acquires the habit of chronic suspicion—a secret apprehension that people spy upon his actions and try to discover his motives. To avoid this he keeps more and more to himself. He does not trust others, reads between the lines of their declarations and detects in them what he imagines is concealed or misrepresented.

Over-active secretiveness is apt to lead to hypocrisy, as when a dishonest man pretends to be honest. Often he acts the part so well that he is not detected. Over-active secretiveness inclines also to intrigue, and according to the strength of the intellectual faculties so will be the plan adopted.

Morbid suspiciousness can arise, particularly in young people, as an exaggeration of a natural disposition to taciturnity and distrustfulness, to seek solitude, to sensitiveness of character, and a hypochondriacal condition. Such people begin to misinterpret everything that happens as intended to do them harm. They suspect everybody and everything, and see hostility everywhere and are constantly on their guard, and the most trifling incidents acquire in their eyes an extraordinary importance. Sometimes they begin to imagine that everybody is looking at them or talks about them. All the words they hear they refer to themselves. Gradually they suspect people of spying and listening at the door and following them when going out. Outside this belief, they may be clear mentally and even brilliant. In consequence of their cleverness, they are often, in their own estimation, under-rated geniuses. Frequently they are innovators or inventors, philosophers or reformers, but without the ability to carry their creations to a practical conclusion. Their want of success may increase their suspicion. They become extremely sensitive regarding the motives of other people, whose kindness even is misinterpreted, and whose silence is regarded as an offence. In reviewing their past life, such men are likely to give a false interpretation to many events. Gradually their delusion becomes more definite, and they accuse persons of ill-will against them. They believe they are the victims of a conspiracy on the part of some public bodies, or secret societies, or even of supernatural agencies. Sometimes their suspicions are directed against particular persons, who do not perceive that they are in danger of becoming victims of revenge. Assaults and actual murder are not uncommon. Others, of a more harmless and inoffensive disposition believing themselves persecuted, fly to the police for protection; and, judging by the number of patients I have seen suffering from this complaint, I imagine that scarcely a day can pass at Scotland Yard when there is not somebody soliciting police aid or giving information about a purely imaginary criminal offence.

Sometimes a man, suffering from this delusion, tries to get right away from the scene and taunts of his persecutors and will be free for a time, but soon his suspicions are again aroused; his enemies have followed him. To be the victim of so much persecution, the patient reasons, he must be some important person; he feels happier now in a delirium of an ambitious nature. Perhaps he is exceptionally gifted, of an exalted position, of great wealth, or a world-saviour, or a prophet, or Providence has some special mission for him. Occasionally he is in love with a lady far above him in social position; sometimes it is only an imaginary person; at other times he pursues some exalted woman with his attention until she seeks the protection of the law from the stranger.

A very common occurrence, of which I have seen a number of examples, is that a person falls in love, but claims the other party to be in love with him. In an innocent way, they may believe the love to be reciprocated, although the object of admiration has never wittingly given any justification for such a supposition. A casual glance, a change of dress or a flower in the buttonhole, is taken to mean that the patient's attentions are favourably received. He addresses poems and love-letters to his supposed sweetheart; and when they are returned and he is told in writing that he can entertain no hope of requital he considers that this is done to try the strength of his affection. Accordingly he becomes more importunate, determined and even threatening. The love of others is not so innocent. Many women imagine occult influences to be exercised on them by their lovers, particularly at night. The belief of sexual outrages committed by means of wireless is a common delusion of females. False accusations and retaliation by blackmail occur. Often these people are so reticent about the affair and their inner thoughts, that they go to prison rather than disclose what passes in their minds. Most of them end in asylums. My observations have led me to the conviction that a good many of these people are addicted to the practice of self-abuse, whether they be men or women, and that they believe their supposed lover, whose image they fancy before them, is guilty of the deed. At first the image is called up voluntarily, but in course of time it becomes fixed, and all sorts of notions are associated with it.

Some people speculate on political affairs and get fixed ideas that the State is mismanaged, that the people are wronged, or else they have imaginary personal grievances, or real but exaggerated, against certain officials. They dwell on these ideas so persistently, although in every other respect reasonable beings, that the brain, so to say, becomes soaked in them and the conduct becomes affected. Such men are continually labouring under a sense of injustice. They are unable to see the world as others see it and have a grievance against some one, whether an individual or public authority. They busy themselves with their grievances. If they go to law, they are never satisfied with the legal decisions, refuse to settle actual wrongs, go from one court to another, and keep bringing one suit after another. The statutes appear to them inadequate, or they see a deep-laid conspiracy to deprive them of their rights. The lawyers they hold incompetent and in collusion with their persecutors. They therefore change their advisers frequently. They are voluminous letter writers and make appeals to persons of prominence, with whom they have not the slightest connection. Finally they become threatening and may commit an offence which turns the pursuer into the defendant. As I have said, granted the premises, the intellect remains unaffected. They remain plausible, converse rationally and coherently, are often exceedingly well-informed, so that they find not a few sympathisers who may aid them in their efforts, and agree with them on the unsatisfactory state of our laws, the prejudice of the judges, and the desirability of reform. Only when we take into consideration the entire life-history of the man do we find the abnormality.

Many people who go through life as eccentric—especially reformers, political enthusiasts, and revolutionaries of society—are possibly only aborted cases of insanity in whom the progress was checked in the early stage, and modified into a sort of crankiness and eccentricity, not pronounced enough for them to be commonly reckoned insane, but sufficient to make them noticeable as odd in behaviour and generally peculiar. They learn, however, to control their conduct and conceal their feelings to a very large extent, so that their real mental condition is not betrayed, except by some habit of writing or speech when they are off their guard.

There are many people in the world who have grievances real and imaginary, and strong over-self-appreciation, yet who are not insane. Many genuine inventors, philosophers, artists, poets, and others, placed in unfavourable circumstances, may have been robbed of the fruits of their works by some unscrupulous person, or else may have failed to attract attention, and, in consequence, formed an unfavourable or delusionary view of the world, against which they take an antagonistic standpoint in consequence of their misfortune. Even the idea of conspiracy may not be totally unfounded, or at least an unreasonable suspicion. How often is an inventor or discoverer, who is more outspoken than is agreeable to established cliques, boycotted by the official authorities and journals ? His opponents might say that he over-estimates his own importance, or deny that there is any such organised obstruction to the recognition of his work, and so the man might be held to be labouring under a delusion; whereas, on the contrary, he may have a sounder and clearer brain than his critics, to be able to hold his own in the face of adverse circumstances, as is often shown when success ultimately comes to him.

The predominant feature in exaggerated ideas of suspicion and persecution is the lack of equilibrium between the intellectual operations on the one hand and the emotions and propensities on the other. The person affected is often remarkable for his shrewdness and argumentative power. His defects are of a moral nature, inasmuch as his emotions and propensities furnish a false basis for his reasoning, and thus cause his brilliant faculties to be at the service of a bad cause—of the instincts and appetites, which owing to the disharmony lead to very extravagant and dangerous acts. Such persons have formed complexes of thoughts which they have associated with feelings that are unjustified, or too intense, or both; in other words, such persons are prejudiced. We are all full of prejudices and ill-founded suspicions: the Tory distrusts the Liberal and Labour politician; the Protestant, the Catholic; the Catholic, the Jew; and so forth. The stronger the feeling associated with the thought, the more persistent the prejudices. In ordinary life the prejudices are limited and do not tend to become elaborated or extreme; sometimes, however, the prejudices pervade the whole personality and gradually usurp the whole range of thought.

The complex may originate in a secret desire which is repugnant to the personality, perhaps because it is incompatible with the individual's general principles or trends of thought. The mind therefore refuses to treat the desire as part of itself, and projects it into some other real or fictitious person, who then becomes an enemy striving to achieve the patient's downfall. Take, for example, the case of the lover fancied by the person in the act of self-abuse. The act itself is disapproved of so strongly, and yet indulged in, that the fanciful person is accused of committing the outrage. This is a case of projection. In its minor degree this mechanism is to be seen in the excuses with which we frequently endeavour to mitigate our moral lapses. We will not acknowledge to ourselves that it was our own ambitions and desires which led to the commission of the fault, but seek to shift the blame to the shoulders of our neighbour. Thus a plain elderly spinster of blameless reputation may complain of the undesirable attentions to which she is subjected by some male acquaintance. She explains that the man is obviously anxious to marry her, and persistently follows her about. Finally certain trifling incidents lead her to write him an indignant letter, or to lodge a complaint with the police. On investigation it is found that the man is not only entirely innocent of the charges levelled against him, but that he has never expressed the least interest in the lady. The explanation is that the lady's sex instincts have been allowed no normal outlet, and have finally become sternly repressed, generally with an exaggerated development in consciousness of the opposite quality. This latter, of course, constitutes the prudery so frequently observed in such cases. The real state of affairs is that the lady is in love with the man but, owing to the repression, the mind will not acknowledge that these ideas and emotions are part of itself, and finds a solution of the conflict by reversing the significance of the desires and projecting them upon their own object. The bearer of the repugnant complex hence appears to the personality as an unwelcome aggressor.

This process also explains how people who possess some fault or deficiency of which they are ashamed are so often notoriously intolerant of that same fault or deficiency in others. Thus the parvenu who is secretly conscious of his own social deficiencies talks much of the "bounders" and "outsiders" whom he observes around him, while the one thing which the muddle-headed man cannot tolerate is a lack of clear thinking in other people. In general it may be said that whenever one encounters an intense prejudice one may with some probability suspect that the individual himself exhibits the fault in question or some closely similar fault.

The man who thinks himself persecuted is out of harmony with his social surroundings and generally harmlessly engrossed with his own personality. He is suspicious of everybody and retires within himself. When suspicion, however, is combined with a certain amount of aggressive tendency, there is danger of retaliation, of the persecuted attacking the supposed persecutor. Medico-psychological literature is full of such cases.

Again, the possibility of head-injury is almost entirely neglected. Not that it is the only or even the principal cause; only that when injury to the head can be proved, there is every chance of recovery. I have seen a large number of cases that developed delusions of suspicion and persecution, after injury to the posterior part of the temporal lobe of the brain, and also a number of cases due to ear disease irritating, or extending to, this part. On removing the cause of the irritation or inflammation, the patients recovered. In some there was a definite history of extreme violence and murderous assaults on the supposed persecutors. For details see my work *In Search of the Soul.*

As according to Freud most psychoses are due to unconscious homosexual tendencies, so " the paranoiac character," according to him, "lies in the fact that as a reaction to the defence against a homosexual wish-phantasy there results a delusion of persecution."

I have found psycho-therapeutic measures combined with constitutional treatment most effective. The chief aim must be to get the patient's thoughts away from himself, and this is best done by such regular, systematic work as necessitates constant attention and employs the powers of observation. The difficulty is that these patients do not admit there is anything wrong with them and direct arguments must be avoided in discussing the matter with them. I have been consulted by a good many persons with delusions of persecution, but only very few of them submitted to treatment and persevered with it. In an institution, however, there should be no difficulty in getting a large number of them restored to mental health.

CHAPTER VI

THEFT AND OTHER MISCONDUCT FOR GAIN

THE propensity to acquire and hoard is another primary propensity. Some animals found it useful not to have to hunt continuously for food, which may prove scarce at certain periods, and began to store up things for future use. Thus developed the hoarding propensity and love of possession, a tendency to lay up provisions for the future. Man similarly acquired the practice of accumulating, in times of plenty, a store of food that should serve for sustenance in times of scarcity. Its obvious advantages soon caused the transfer of the desire and the practice to other things than food. Man not only stored up provisions for the winter, but he acquired property of every sort and kind for all his life and for his posterity; until, in the course of ages, it culminated in the practice of accumulating money, the symbol and potentiality of acquiring most things that are regarded as desirable. Having started as a means to the further end of security against future want, it has now, by the process of anticipation of motive, become an end in itself, and we have the familiar spectacle of men who have already accumulated money in excess of any possible need still going on with the accumulation for the mere sake of accumulating. From food and money, the practice has overflowed, by an easy process of transference, to other things, some useful, many useless, and we now see people accumulating book-plates, postage stamps, and all kinds of queer things, merely to satisfy the secondary instinct of accumulation.

The tendency to acquire varies in different people; the ability to do so depends on the intellect and other requisite qualities. The hoarding instinct is one of the strongest and most general impulses of our nature, and, in fact, is the origin of wealth, by the tendency which it produces to acquire for the mere pleasure of possessing. For the sake of gratifying his desire to acquire, one man saves where others spend; one man is diligent, and another speculates, to get rich quickly. Like other propensities, acquisitiveness is liable to become morbidly exaggerated—to cupidity, greed, miserliness, and dishonest acquisition.

The love of wealth, as distinct from the desire for objects of immediate gratification, in which it undoubtedly takes its rise, is an object of future gratification, and therefore requires foresight. First we provide for our own wants, next for those connected with us, and ultimately wealth is amassed without any regard for its future use. The amassing itself becomes a pleasure for its own sake. Its ill effects are a grasping and covetous disposition; its good effects, the stimulation of frugality and industry. When the desire for the accumulation of money has become a man's ruling principle, and he exhibits it on all occasions, he is called covetous or avaricious.

For the crowd, the idea of happiness never extends beyond a limited circle of immediate and tangible satisfactions which can be bought with money. In order to succeed, all means are justified, and success is the sole measure of the value of actions. Success under its most brutal form, which is monetary success, has almost become the exclusive object of universal endeavour. The collective ideal is the same as the individual ideal—to get rich as soon as possible, and by every available means. Admiration and respect are accorded to those who have succeeded financially. Fraudulent people frequently succeed because of their knowledge of mankind, especially because of the knowledge of the most common weakness: to get rich quickly without doing any work for it.

The desire to become rich destroys the capacity for happiness when the riches are obtained; but there continues a ceaseless activity. The governing classes are no longer the higher classes, and what remains of the old aristocracy has but little concern in maintaining its intellectual supremacy, or in constituting itself as a social force and setting an effective example. The only effective aristocracy that survives is that of money—a mere plutocracy—and it cares for nothing save augmenting its wealth or spending it without intelligence.

Love of possession is a natural disposition implanted in the human organisation, and dishonesty is only the result of the absence of controlling motives. In the child the acquisitive propensity shows itself most naturally. The child will seize everything and appropriate what does not belong to it. In a sense, the child is a natural thief—he grasps everything about him that his primitive instincts impel him to crave. Fear of punishment finally deters him. If he is normal, this is replaced later by consciousness of his true relation to his environment and his duty to those around him, i.e. by incipient altruism. In some children this is slow of development ; in others it never develops.

All human beings are trained for gain; that is to say, they all have to acquire the ability to earn a livelihood and to a certain extent the ability to administer the means. The due and proper administration of means requires, in the first place, that a proper proportion should be observed among the various objects of expenditure. Expenditure in excess is prodigality ; inadequately, it is miserliness. By prodigality I mean the lack of will to forgo the immediate enjoyment of spending, at the inevitable and foreseen cost of future embarrassment. The " mean " man will spend sufficient money on himself, but grudge his fair share of common expenditure.

Cupidity and greed are caused by general selfishness combined with this propensity. Penuriousness is caused by the activity of acquisitiveness in a timid or weak man. The pleasure of avarice consists in accumulating and hoarding up treasures; in computing and gloating over them; in a feeling of the power which they bestow; and likewise in the consciousness of the possession of the means, though there be no disposition to employ them for the purpose of enjoyment. Envy is directed towards those who already, or at least as we conceive, enjoy something more and better, either internal or external gifts, than belongs to ourselves. When the acquiring propensity is combined with cautiousness, such a person will save rather than speculate. A person with only poor acquisitive propensity desires money more as a means than as an end. He may be industrious but lack economy, and is likely to show disinterestedness in pecuniary matters.

A man may acquire property dishonestly, as by thieving, without love of possession; and a man may be moral and yet grasping. There are many rogues who are not very acquisitive and who readily part with what they have stolen; that is to say, they are dishonest but not selfish; and there are many avaricious men who are sternly honest. In moderation, not out of proportion to the other impulses, we see persons not grasping, but with a conservative and economical tendency towards property, and a disposition to take good care of everything they possess. They waste nothing, but they are not necessarily selfish or very eager in the pursuit of wealth.

The weakness of human nature in the direction of theft and swindling is most evident at the two extremes of such crimes—petty thefts and big thefts. Persons who would be horrified were they to be called thieves and swindlers will misappropriate certain articles, like a book or an umbrella, without a tremor. Big frauds within the law may bring honours to the man.

Some people, though perfectly sane in every other respect, have morbid impulses whenever there is any temptation to pilfer. Such impulsive stealing has certain points which are of importance to know. The person may be rich and by no means ungenerous with his money, and may yet appropriate articles which are worthless in themselves and of no practical use to himself, the articles being generally of the same kind—handkerchiefs, ties, watch-chains, scarf-pins, books; moreover, the stolen goods are not parted with for personal gain, but are accumulated uselessly. These are the points of difference between kleptomania and theft. Kleptomania is a much abused term. In everyday life its diagnosis revolves largely around the social standing of the thief. Kleptomania is frequently used as an excuse for people who are really thieves, except that they are of such social standing that the value of the article pilfered is really nothing to them. Such people are honest as a rule, but they simply cannot withstand the temptation of goods that are displayed on open counters, when they believe themselves unobserved. Women particularly are given to petty thieving, as proved by the frequency with which articles of value disappear from the cloak-rooms of fashionable functions. It is for them that detectives are needed in drapery stores and at exhibitions of wedding presents. Their discovery and public exposure generally effects a cure, and they exercise self-control ever afterwards, unless they are professional or born thieves.

There is another class of people who do not actually steal, but have the impulse to do so. They struggle with their inclination till they nearly faint. What they suffer from is really " fear of stealing," and their suffering is quite as bad as of those subjects of morbid fears with whom we shall deal in a succeeding chapter. Most of the cases I have seen were wealthy men, frequently sons of self-made men, who complained of this fear of pilfering whenever they saw articles of value openly displayed, especially jewellery. They are really honest men, for they seek medical advice in time; different from the so-called kleptomaniacs, who do not come for treatment, but to get expert assistance after the deed to prove their irresponsibility.

People on the borderland of insanity sometimes steal, embezzle, defraud, and it may be the very offence that calls attention to the state of their mind. Thus in hypomania, the early stage of mania proper, the patient sometimes steals whatever he can lay hands on, but the articles stolen are often thrown away as soon as they are in his possession, and he steals almost openly. General paralytics, in the early stage of the disease, not infrequently steal without reflection, though sometimes with ingenuity, as a rule any article that takes their fancy. They also enter recklessly into speculations and commit frauds of every kind, generally neglecting ordinary precautions. They would not forge signatures, but they draw cheques for amounts which they never had or are never likely to have at their banks. One of my patients defrauded his employers, and was not discovered until after his death when the account-books were examined. His employers brought an action to recover the money from the estate he left. In the latter stages of general paralysis, which, however, are generally seen in asylums only, they again steal, but this time under the delusion that everything belongs to them. They then appropriate all sorts of articles, hoard and conceal them, and immediately afterwards lose all recollection of them.

Stealing without reflection and merely to satisfy their animal instinct is common among a certain class of the weak-minded. They will purloin whatever takes their fancy. Sometimes they display a considerable amount of ingenuity and low cunning in their methods of procedure. There is rarely any difficulty in diagnosing intellectual deficiency. But there are others, intellectually normal or even gifted, but who lack all moral appreciation—the so-called "morally weak-minded"—who easily yield to temptation. Their mental state can be diagnosed only by investigating their entire history, from infancy onwards, and by showing the co-existence of other and permanent defects of morality. (See Chapter X.)

Among other perverted manifestations of the hoarding propensity, particularly in oncoming insanity, we have, on the one hand, the patient who fears loss of property and destitution, or thinks he is already ruined; on the other hand, the parsimonious man who suddenly launches out into endless extravagance, giving orders for motor-cars, jewellery, and other luxuries, which, as already mentioned, he has often not the means to pay for, or else makes imprudent investments, or is given to impracticable business ventures.

Kleptomania occurs also in the mental disorder which sometimes accompanies pregnancy, in the clouded consciousness of hysteria, and sometimes in the semi-conscious state following an epileptic fit. Occasionally a fit may be replaced by a temporary state of clouded consciousness (see Chapter IV), when conduct not natural to the ordinary character of the patient may be manifested. I have treated several cases of epileptics, who committed robberies, for which they were sent to prison, and who in the intervals were conducting themselves as men of the highest character. Yet after a time, in one case every three months, they changed for a few hours or days to what one can only describe as a secondary personality, and got again into trouble. It is essential to prove previously existing major or minor epilepsy, or at least epileptic family history, and I have found that treating these character-changes exactly as I do ordinary fits, the patients make a good recovery.

It may be as well to mention here that, according to the orthodox Freudian school, "kleptomania arises from ungratified sexual instinct." Thus "women who have not the courage to commit a sin against morality will steal some article, which is of no value to them, as the symbolic fulfilment of a forbidden action, whereby the symbolic significance of the stolen article very often reveals the true nature of the instinctive action" (Stekel: *Disguises of Love*). We may well defer our opinion on this explanation until a psychoanalyst of the ultra-Freudian kind, who sees "sex" in every abnormality, will give evidence in defence of a lady kleptomaniac. We shall then hear what the judge will have to say on the defence that the article stolen symbolically gratified the lady's sexual longings.

Genuine thieves may be classified into those who rob because they are too idle to work honestly; those who rob because legitimate labour does not reward them with a sufficiency to enable them to satisfy their various passions; and those who rob by instinct and who may come from classes who are neither idle nor poor. A momentary temptation may turn the honest man in whom the propensity is large, into a thief. Take the cashier who sees his principal invest money in a speculative enterprise, which is supposed to be a certainty. He is envious and wishes he had ever so little money to put into the same speculation. In a weak moment he "borrows" from his principal's cash-box the necessary sum, which he feels sure he will be able to repay. Unfortunately the market goes down and the principal covers himself from loss by buying more stock at the lower price. His clerk borrows more money to do the same. If in the end the whole speculation is a failure, the principal has lost only a certain sum of money; but his clerk is discovered to be a thief, loses his situation and may have to go to prison. If employers would only realise that every man is a potential thief, they would organise such supervision over accounts, cash, and securities, that no sane man could feel tempted, because of the certainty of immediate detection. Even great length of service is no definite guarantee, where the temptation is always present.

The professional thief is a natural gambler. He is occupied chiefly in estimating the dangers of his occupation and the liability of getting caught, and, if caught, his chances of punishment. The laws are to him simply impediments thrown in his way by the Upper World to prevent him from getting his living. He often has the highest possible respect for his own branch of the profession of crime. If one were to argue with him, he would probably point to the man who amasses great wealth by grinding down the poor, or cornering the necessities of life; or he would point to the unscrupulous banker, or dishonest stock-jobber, who robs his credulous dupes by the score by watering stocks; and we should be told that the world in these cases calls the robbery good business instinct. On the other hand, the burglar might point to the action of nations: whenever a civilised nation has seen something it wanted to steal, it has found serious flaws in the people's refinement, education, and religion, and particularly in their mode of handling their own property, and found some excuse for the occupation of their country either by civil means or by war.

Finally there is the thief whose over-active propensity is due to head-injury. I have published a number of cases involving the anterior-superior temporal region (in the work already quoted) and recorded complete recovery after surgical operation.

I have also had a number of young men brought to me, of respectable parentage, who were addicted to stealing, but who had escaped punishment so far, though in one case the wrong person was accused and allowed to go to prison. Appropriate psychotherapy, as described in Chapter XII, achieved a lasting moral change. Only the congenitally moral feeble-minded and the professional thief are without hope.

Swindling, to be successful, must be done on a large scale and requires exact knowledge. Forgery demands skill and education. Long firms, bogus company promoting, and blackmailing require characteristics and knowledge that only a cunning brain does possess. Many of the jewel-thieves possess skill, if not actual intellect. And all these forms of dishonesty betray a criminal mind and criminal intention. Many years ago, a doctor, whose practice lay chiefly among a certain class of questionable people, took me into a thieves' den, really quite a decent restaurant in one of the side streets off Piccadilly, where I made the acquaintance among others of an American, who was then the greatest expert pickpocket in London. He was a gentlemanly young fellow not to be differentiated from ordinary smart young fellows about town. I wanted to study his head, but he would keep his hat on. The only things I could notice were his slender, nervous build, his deft, restless, long fingers, and the mobility of his eyes, which seemed to look at one and at the same time round the corner. A few weeks later I was a week-end guest at a country mansion, where for some reason a well-known Scotland Yard detective visited, with whom I had interesting chats. I told him of the thieves' den, which he professed to know. But on my questioning him why he did not have the place raided, his only reply was: "That is not our way." Apparently these men could not be apprehended unless some one complained of missing property.

Lastly, I should like to mention "gambling," firstly, because it is a universal vice, and secondly, because it occurs sometimes at the onset of insanity, in hypomania and general paralysis of the insane. Gambling arises from the wish to make money without having to work for it, and may be compared to drug addiction: once started, it grows on one. Even if money is made by it, the winner rarely gains anything, except temporarily, for money thus lightly come by goes lightly. On the other hand, the loser often not only ruins himself, but drags his family with him. Moreover, gambling is one of the commonest incentives to crime, especially embezzlement.

CHAPTER VII

THE FEAR OF CONSEQUENCES

DEFENCELESS animals and animals recognising the superiority of the enemy instinctively take to flight. The struggle for existence has exposed them, especially the weak, to continual risk. The consciousness of past dangers has caused them to fear the enemy and, when possible, to run away from him. Generally speaking, the unfamiliar arouses the fear instinct; for what is unfamiliar may be a menace to life. The emotion of fear has its object in nature to make the animal apprehend danger. The power to experience fear is necessary for self-preservation. Animals which must receive actual injury before experiencing pain are clearly inferior to those which experience emotion-pain before the injury is actually received. Fear is perhaps more essential to the human species than to the brute creatures, for we do not possess the same facility of avoiding danger by rapid flight, or of concealing ourselves by what may be called instinctive stratagems.

Fear constitutes an insurance for the preservation

of the animal or species by compelling withdrawal from situations that threaten injury or death, or by prohibiting approach to such situations. The effect of fear upon the system proves its uncontrollable influence. The sudden stopping of the heart-beat and respiration, and the paralysis of movement in which it sometimes finds expression, are due to the impulse of concealment; hurried respiration and pulse, and the frantic bodily efforts, by which it is more commonly expressed, are due to the impulse of flight.

The objects of fear vary according to the individual constitution. Each man has his special fears, as his fear is combined with other sentiments; thus there is fear of loss of money, power, reputation, and many other things besides life.

Fear incites us to avoid, or flee from, dangers. When escape, however, is impracticable, the emotion may change and the individual will often be driven to the most fierce and desperate resistance; thus even the greatest cowards have sometimes acquired the fame of heroes. We cannot feel fear and anger at the same time; but anger may follow fear. The weaker animals fight better when they experience fear and are driven to be at bay, and men often fight better when they are rightly afraid and have justice on their side.

Normally, fear incites the intellect to produce prudence and circumspection; when deficient it causes recklessness and carelessness, and the danger is not seen until escape is impossible. In excess it causes indecision, cowardice, and, in some, such a depression of spirits, that with the slightest misfortune they fall into despair and think life no longer worth living.

Courage frequently means blindness to danger, a lack of imagination to realise the horrors of a distant catastrophe. A man who is mentally alert and well informed, and therefore able to gauge pretty accurately dangers he is called upon to face, is not likely to distinguish himself for physical courage. On the other hand, the naturally timid, if they possess the higher faculties, may be stimulated by duty, honour, pride, so that in many instances they become bold and successful warriors. The most delicate and effeminate in body, through the ascendant influence of their moral nature, have faced dangers and borne sufferings under which naturally stouter hearts and firmer nerves quailed. Fear will oftentimes spring rather from mistaken judgment than from any absolute deficiency of courage.

Fear, because of its anticipation of consequences, is not only an essential instinctive feeling for the protection of the individual, but it is also a powerful agent in the preservation of social order. A child with little moral sense but large fear may, from dread of punishment, avoid telling falsehoods, until with years the habit of speaking the truth has become a second nature. Fear is also the basis of morality among many uncultured people. They do not steal, because they fear the gaol, and they do not murder, because they are afraid of the gallows. It is already a moral advance when a man has large domestic affections and will not steal, not because he fears the gaol, but because it would give pain to his mother, wife, or sisters. We all behave ourselves, in a measure, for " fear " of public opinion.

Fear is a revived experience of past painful experiences. It is fear that urges the organism to avoid a previous danger, and therefore, fear has a definite biological value. The fear of solitude, of being without protection, of vast distances or of open spaces ; the fear of enclosed places or of great heights or of darkness—all of use to our ancestors—are notable instances of inherited instincts that may be revived under stress through pathological conditions.

All fear can be traced back to fear of the unknown, no matter whether it is bankruptcy, insanity, of physical collapse or death itself.

This instinct must be sublimated, not repressed. It must be directed under the control of reason into proper channels. Wrongly used, it makes life a misery. Fear, under the guidance of reason, inspires action, stimulates effort. Fear of poverty spurs us on to greater exertion and further toil ; fear of disease makes us cautious, active, and alert. A healthy fear of indulgence will lead to prudence, industry, and thrift.

Owing to the comparative safety afforded by

modern civilisation, there is a superfluity of fear, and the instinct remains in man in a greater degree than is necessary for the preservation of his life. This superfluity is apt to find an outlet in ways which are futile. People either fear immoderately things in regard to which a certain measure of fear is both reasonable and natural, or they fear things which ought not to be feared at all. The result is that our lives are filled with needless worry and anxiety, often to the ruin of our health and to the undoing of our peace of mind.

Apprehensiveness, which is natural to all of us, in some people is greatly exaggerated. They are either congenitally over-apprehensive, or an exaggerated apprehensiveness is acquired by habits which lower the tone of the nervous system. These people manifest the emotion of anxiety upon the least pretext, and from this morbid susceptibility arises a constant state of uneasiness. They are subject to doubts, hesitations, fears concerning the most ordinary circumstances and acts of life. Such persons cannot meet the ordinary ills of life with a normal degree of fortitude; they grow discouraged with the smallest failures, magnify every obstacle and profess inability to surmount it. They create painful emotions by representing to their minds ideas of danger, or of evil or fear. They are easily discouraged, shy, timid, and fearful, and have lost confidence in themselves and their own ability. The ego will often become intensely exaggerated, and although the patient may be diffident in manner, still he is extremely self-conscious and shy, and he often labours under the idea that, whether at a party or in the street or at any place of public amusement, he is the observed of all observers. He neglects his social duties, deliberately retires into solitude, and declares himself unable to manage his affairs. The habit of looking at the gloomy side of things is easily formed, and, once acquired, it becomes very forceful. Mental depression has a contracting effect on the personality, tends to keep the thoughts in one groove, on one set of ideas or objects, and that a narrow one.

Emotional obsessions, generally of fear, are readily formed and become more and more fixed. These fears are known to the subject as morbid and irrational, but still they dominate his conduct. Sometimes the natural repugnance associated with certain acts is enormously exaggerated; sometimes the fixed ideas consist in the representation of the impossibility of accomplishing certain acts, a representation which is translated into a real impossibility. Sometimes these fears originate with some special unpleasant experience, or the mere reading of one in a sensational newspaper paragraph. In all cases it is the weakened inhibition that is at fault. Some people are drenched with the anxious emotion, dealing with the past, feeling regrets, remorse, scruples; or with the future, leading them to indecision and apprehension. Some fear objects, some open or enclosed places, some living beings. The fear of others is in the range of ideas, producing an obsession of doubt. In others fear affects the will, i.e. volition; they do not wish to act. In some execution of an act is affected, as when the subject cannot make his decision pass into a motor act. In the one there is a non-willingness; in the other a non-ability.

Again, in others, there is a fear of disease, sometimes to such an extent as to prevent the patient following his calling. This may persist for years without in any way producing mental decay and without spreading, as it were, to the other mental functions. A typical case is that of a middle-aged man who ought to work for his living, yet who does nothing but consider his bodily feelings. He notes everything, from his pulse to his urine and his stools. He is inclined to weigh all his food, and he guards himself against every change in the weather. He exacts the utmost care and attention from wife and family, leading them a life of misery.

Besides these general hypochondriacs we meet with others who have some limitation to their apprehensive ideas. Such a man may be haunted by the idea that he is suffering from malignant disease of the stomach; while all the time he is perfectly aware that there is no foundation for this suspicion and that no symptom of the dreadful disease is actually present. He does not, in fact, really believe that he has cancer, but he cannot banish the idea from his mind, and he needs constantly to reassure himself of its erroneous character. It is this absence of a definite false belief that constitutes the essential distinction between an obsession and a delusion.

Such patients love to consult numerous doctors and can talk for hours about their ailment. I remember a commercial traveller, very loquacious about his complaint, which he said prevented him from following his calling. I could not help telling him that if he had been equally eloquent in praising his goods to a likely customer, he might have sold something in the meantime. Such patients require firm treatment, but unfortunately their people humour them too much. It is mistaken sympathy which enforces the idea of sickness and incapacity still further on their mind. With proper psychotherapy they soon get well.

The instinct of fear is normal to mankind, but instead of getting moderated as we grow older, it may be rendered over-active by faulty education and disturbing events of social life. It may also become morbid in one direction only by particular incidents or by particular objects and states, and thus become associated with definite situations, giving rise to morbid fears. Often the fears of early childhood, fostered by frights, scares, religious and social injunctions, with the consequent dread of failure and fear of punishment, remain subconscious and get repressed in the unconscious, yet continue to influence conscious thought and feeling whenever similar situations arise, or brain and body get fatigued.

Whereas the normal person apprehensive of danger will ask himself, "What can I *do* to be safe?" the abnormal person asks, "What shall I *avoid* to be safe?" Thus arise the various phobias. Often the dreams of such a person reveal in a symbolic form the anxiety, painful memory, or repressed experience.

Another theory of the origin of morbid fears is that they are really symptomatic of unconscious desires. When a person experiences a desire which, for some reason or other, he does not wish to feel, perhaps because he thinks it wrong or wicked, he represses it into his unconscious and it becomes replaced in consciousness by its opposite, namely, fear. He then suffers from morbid fear of any situation which tends to remind him of his unconscious aspiration, even symbolically. In some cases, on the other hand, the fear is traceable to some situation, consciously forgotten but remembered by the unconscious, in which the patient did not react emotionally at the time, so that, as it would appear, there is a certain amount of fear floating about loose, so to speak, which tends to attach to any situation resembling the original, even remotely.

In these cases, morbid fears are the external expression of internal wishes—that the feared event may not happen. When the underlying wish is of a repressed kind, a phobia frequently replaces it in consciousness; the phobia being a protective fear built up by a process of projection to guard against outbursts of anxiety. It follows as a natural consequence that such fears cannot be removed by appeals to the patient's conscious processes, for the cause of them does not lie there. The conscious process that evokes the anxiety is not the cause, but only the exciting agent; it is merely a signal that acts by arousing through association the real cause, which is entirely unconscious.

Freud and some of his followers claim on the basis of their psychoanalytic experiences that under certain circumstances sexual excitations arise that cannot follow their natural course of leading to either physical gratification or conscious desire for such; being deflected by their aim, they manifest themselves mentally as morbid anxiety, physically as the bodily accompaniment of the same. I have found this true only in one form—in *coitus interruptus*—and then it produces definite unmistakable symptoms. But when *all* forms of morbid anxiety are claimed by Freudians as derived from—or as a reaction against—repressed sex instinct, I cannot agree.

Morbid fears are common in neurasthenia, hysteria, and the so-called anxiety-neuroses. Fear as to health and apprehension of disease is the main condition of hypochondriasis. Terrifying hallucinations occur in alcoholic delirium. Unreasonable excessive apprehension and vague feelings of anxiety are common in melancholics; their whole life is tinctured with sadness, anxiety casts a gloom over all their thoughts and actions. They can find no pleasure in anything, and feel as if their body were fixed in the place where they are; or else they may be so agitated as to run about in violent despair. Their delusions, if they have any, are not the cause of their disorder, but are mere efforts on their part to explain their misery. On the other hand, fear and anxiety, caution and prudence, may be diminished or lost as a consequence of mental disorder and lead to actions resulting in the ruin of the patient and his family.

Some people have a constitutional disposition to fear readily, to look at the dark side of things and to be apprehensive, often without cause or with insufficient cause, and they may contemplate suicide at the prospect of future misery. But it is not misfortune that drives them to it; for there are millions of people who bear with cheerfulness disappointment, loss of wealth, loss of husband, wife, children, friends, of health, character, or social position, but do not dream of ending their lives.

Nervousness and emotional instability are often due to unusual timidity, especially in children. They become deficient in self-confidence, in aggressiveness, even in the capacity of enjoyment, and are likely to grow up shy and self-conscious. All morbidly shy persons are extremely self-conscious, and very apt, especially in early life, to lack self-reliance; but they may nevertheless have a very good opinion of themselves and are not infrequently self-opinionated—tenacious of view and of purpose. The very shy persons will sometimes put forward their views with great modesty, and one might fancy that they could easily be argued out of them, whereas it will be found that they obstinately cling to them. Speaking broadly, we may say that shyness consists essentially in a state of extreme sensitiveness and morbid self-consciousness of one's personal characteristics, physical or mental, in relation to the opinions of others, and sometimes of one's history or station in life. It finds a fruitful ally in a too active imagination, and may render life a burden. Excessive self-consciousness causes the speaker, the actor, the musician, not sure of themselves, to watch their movements, which should be automatic, and thus to impair their efficiency. It may literally paralyse movement and speech.

Both diffidence and shyness are produced by a sense of unworthiness or inferiority in the individual, quite irrespective of the estimate of others. But shyness does not necessarily proceed from even a sense of moral, mental, or physical deficiency. That the shy person is not necessarily distrustful of his powers is shown by the fact that he may become aggressive in his writings. Some of our most self-assertive and combative writers have been shy men. The shyness in their case manifests itself only in the fear of meeting other people, in whose presence they feel a strain. A man with large esteem of his physical and intellectual personality may yet be a shy man. He is over-sensitive to criticism and anticipates it keenly. He is afraid not merely of adverse criticism; he is also shy of praise and blushes all over. Shyness, then, is more often anxiety to appear well in the eyes of others. The greater the shyness, the more awkward the person, the more frequent slips and accidents, which further aggravate the complaint. That is how shy persons trip on a rug entering a room, upset a glass, or draw attention to themselves by some other mishap. The mere recollection of the accident revives the feeling and intensifies it.

Shyness is natural at puberty, and is then the outcome of the growth of the sex instinct. In young women, one takes it perhaps as more or less natural. Men afflicted with this complaint feel it more keenly. A shy person may blush, be confused, have tremors or restless movements, have a nervous laugh and a foolish expression, with the eyes glancing restlessly in all directions. He sometimes tries to hide his discomfort. In consequence of these feelings, he isolates himself from society and even from ordinary companions sometimes, and becomes a lonely man, with all the evils of self-contemplation, self-introspection, eccentricity, etc., that are apt to develop in the recluse.

Shyness—that is, the fear of meeting other people—may lead to strain in their presence and to nervous affections of speech, especially stuttering. Stuttering is a bad habit; it is not a speech defect, for stutterers can speak perfectly well so long as they are alone.

The stutterer's spasm varies from case to case; no two persons stutter alike. Again, it varies from sentence to sentence, from word to word. Finally, it varies from time to time and from circumstance to circumstance. In very bad cases there may be a temporary spasm of the muscles round the mouth. I had once within the same week two cases of stutterers suffering from spasm of exactly opposite nature; one on starting to speak opened his mouth wide and appeared unable to close it, the other pressed his lips firmly together and seemed unable to separate them. Curiously the latter one I got well; with the first one I failed.

Sometimes a shy disposition and morbid fears arise from bad habits of a sexual nature, which have to be corrected. But they are not invariably due to such causes, as the Freudians believe. Frequently the principal symptom to be noticed is a lack of nervous energy, and any method which will restore or increase the tone of the nervous system will restore or increase self-confidence, and when feeling again a strong man the morbid fears vanish; but if not entirely, then is the time for such psychotherapy as will establish confidence in the presence of others, for the teaching of mental discipline, and the re-education of the character.

CHAPTER VIII

SEXUAL PERVERSENESS

THE sexual instinct is the strongest instinct in nature, and was not given for pleasure but for the purpose of procreation. In the higher animals the pleasurable performance of the functions is purely secondary. Were it not necessary, in order that a given species should not forget the function altogether, the pleasure would not exist. When the object of the sexual act, impregnation, has been accomplished, both act and desire should cease. In all species save man, they cease in the female. In monogamous lower animals they also cease in the male. The persistence in the human female is probably the outgrowth of woman's response to the physiological demands of man. The persistence of sexual desire in women during pregnancy and lactation and after the menopause is artificial. It has no longer a natural object.

Unless it be claimed that the sexual function was primarily designed for human pleasure, it must be admitted that man is polygamous by nature. The instinctive tendency of the male towards polygamy is one of the conditions against which normal men who would be moral have to fight. It is one of the fundamental causes of sexual vice. Once social inhibitions are removed, man drops only too readily into his natural rôle of woman-hunter. Man, without his ideals of femininity, would rapidly degenerate.

Woman becomes polyandrous only as a result of disease, degeneracy, or vicious surroundings. Her natural bent is not towards polyandry. She has not that to fight. If she had to combat natural polyandrous instincts as well as man's polygamous instincts and acquired depravity, her position in the moral scale would be low indeed. Social custom is repressive of sexual indulgence in woman. She is normally less sexual from the standpoint of pleasure alone. Indeed, a large proportion of women are frigid; some remain so only until sexually trained by man. Sin is blacker in woman than in man, simply because she is by nature purer and has farther to fall.

Virtue once lost, it may be readily understood that the one great barrier to a life of shame has been swept away. While in the majority of cases the man is at fault, there is a certain class of women whose seduction is a literal impossibility. There may be a first offence, but a seduction, never. There is a numerous class in which the woman is more than compliant, or even enacts the active rôle in the so-called seduction. The superior woman falls in the first instance, not through immorality, but through the power of a great love. However, seduction under promise of marriage, without its consummation, is comparatively exceptional. In most cases, probably, the woman falls from grace without a word having been said about matrimony on either side. Matrimony is here the woman's afterthought; sometimes not until she is *enceinte*.

One of the results of illicit sexuality is abortion. It is a cruel law which keeps the child born before marriage illegitimate. It has a bad effect on the child. It is branded with infamy as a bastard. The bastardy laws protect a woman who has been betrayed and open the road for thousands of others who entice a dozen men each and blackmail the lot. Considering the amount of illicit intercourse, rape of women is very rare indeed. Flirtation and provocative conduct, i.e. tacit if not actual consent, is generally the prelude to intercourse. Most women are able to protect themselves, and even when their indiscretion delivers them up to the mercy of a man, there are avenues of escape to the woman who is not herself excited. If the man is presumably of her own station in life, she can appeal to his better feelings. Thus a man who was carried away by his instincts to make an assault on the girl with whom he kept company confessed to me that she saved herself by the exclamation: "How would you like this to happen to your sister?"

Well-developed young women are very prone to

have an unusual amount of sex feeling and sex consciousness, and just such women are regarded as especially attractive by the opposite sex. Such women exercise often a peculiar fascination over men, and, if depraved and vicious, they lead the men, infatuated with them, on the road to a criminal career, should they have not the means to gratify their multitudinous whims. One of my patients was a woman of that type, of very good family, for whom at least half a dozen men committed suicide. She was a prepossessing woman, so fascinating and enchanting, and with such expensive tastes, that men, to keep in her favour, committed frauds and defalcations, and when discovered were so overcome with shame and remorse that they made an end to their existence.

The undoing of criminals by women offsets to a certain extent their occasional malign influence. Once the woman in whom the criminal is interested is located, his capture is almost a foregone conclusion. Sooner or later he will be found in her society.

Actual prostitutes do not come within the observation of the psychological physician. They are a class apart, a good many of them having been trained to their life from childhood. Anyhow, a large proportion begin their career of shame before they have attained their majority. They adopt the life from choice, and remain in it from choice. If they are of better-class descent, they sometimes marry after all, and not infrequently become unassailable models of domestic virtue. The inebriate, poverty-stricken prostitute is not ashamed either. If she repents, she does so because she would like to do better from the standpoint of physical comfort. The high-class courtesan rarely wishes to reform, so long as she is in demand. The lower-class prostitute rarely can be reformed, although she may express a wish to be. Much does depend on their physical attraction, and whether they are already contaminated with venereal disease.

The average moralist, accepting marriage as a divine institution instead of what it really is—a conventionalised regulation of sexual love, a civil, business, and social contract—is dominated entirely by the dogma of indissoluble marriage, "until death us do part." Unfortunately for the philosophy of such moralists the divinity of marriage is sadly masked by the fact that, whatever it is in theory, in practice it is a human institution in which the contracting parties are not demigods but human beings, with all the fleshly attributes thereunto belonging. These human beings are possessed of certain animal traits, besides the intellectual attributes that are distinctively human. Marriage is not a question of a lovers' evening out; it is a steady and intimate association, day in and day out, which only compatibles can face without disaster. Neither man nor woman knows one another until they spend a night together. Physical incompatibility exists far oftener than is generally supposed. A single hour may shatter all the pre-marital ideals. On the other hand, the demand for congenial companionship is greater than it has been heretofore, and, as the test can only be made after marriage, mental incompatibility has necessarily become more prominent in matrimony.

Men dream less of ideals than women. Many persons go through life without meeting their ideal. Some realise what they have missed; the majority, fortunately, do not, and are perfectly happy in their ignorance. When the ideal comes in a legitimate manner, or when the conception of the ideal does not exist, and the partner selected is sufficiently near the physical correlative, everything goes smoothly. Should the ideal appear at an inopportune moment, trouble arises—trouble that the whole world recognises and blindly explains on moral grounds.

Where the physical conditions of married persons are absolutely harmonious, mental incompatibility is unusual. The woman wants to be spiritually gratified more than physically; the man frequently just the reverse. In most cases of marital infelicity it is safe to say that the husband is at fault. There is a very cogent reason for this. He has usually a physical standard in mind based upon previous experience. While the glamour of early married life lasts, he is satisfied with the situation. When satiety arrives, as it usually does sooner or later, he begins to recall memories of past experience, in the light of which the physical charms of the wife begin to pale. Once the sexual will-o'-the-wisp begins flitting about in his brain, he discovers physical incompatibility, and resumes the chase after elusive past sexual impressions that his marriage temporarily interrupted.

The question as to whether morality is bettered or made worse by lax divorce laws is still an open one. If either the man or the woman has made a serious mistake, matrimony is hell. There should be no law, human or divine, compelling people to live in a hell on earth. To compel them to do so is wrong, both to the individual and to society. It is in itself immoral, and leads to immorality outside the pale of matrimony. It may lead to murder and to suicide. It is bad for the children that grow up in a vicious home and have their training neglected. There is much opposition to making divorce easier, but none to the present system of allowing anybody capable of asking for a licence, in person or by proxy, to marry. Until marriage is made more difficult, and properly regulated, altruism would appear to lie in the direction of making divorce easier. But divorce is not merely a question of morals; it is also a question of economics. What is to become of the wife and mother? Therefore the man is bound to provide for her, as long as she keeps decent and until she marries, though the separation is by mutual agreement. Mere separation without ability to re-marry leads to immorality.

In men there is often a marked inability to attain

adjustment to the other sex, and especially a shrinking from marriage and an inability to fall in love. This is often due to their having no experience of good women, and having intimate knowledge only of prostitutes. Having gratified their instinct without the refining influences of love, they are unable to bestow the combination on the women to whom they are married. Consequently there is sexual gratification in wedlock without tenderness and regard.

Just as in the man who has been addicted to excessive masturbation or homosexual habits or other perversity there is often impotence for the natural act, so sometimes in the man who has had intercourse only with prostitutes there may be incapacity with a woman who makes no sexual advances to him. Marriages are often annulled on that ground, though the husband may claim he is competent with other women. On the other hand, there are women very sympathetic, if not loving, who are sexually absolutely frigid, almost anæsthetic; others, hypersensitive, suffer from spasmodic contraction of the muscles, preventing consummation; in others there is some disorder due to anæmia or other disturbance; so that man is not always to blame.

In some women the impulse to devilment and foolishness in order to get some variety in life is very strong, leading them first to flirtations, then to little disloyalties, and finally to adultery. That such indiscretions are not a thousand times more frequent is merely due to the accident that the right man is not at hand during these so-called weak moments. Sometimes it is negligence on the part of the husband; but frequently, when it is not wickedness, it is lack of understanding on the part of the wife that the husband as the constant companion cannot match in attention and devotion the man who makes it his business to impress and win a woman during a meeting or visit of an hour or so.

The husband is rarely jealous without good ground; the wife often unreasonably so. The husband may be sexually weak or cold, and the wife misinterprets this. She thinks the husband has a mistress or two, and begins by reading the impressions on his blotting-pads. She spies on him, empties his pockets, and even follows him to his office unexpectedly, thinking to convict him. The unreasonable jealousy of the wife, generally combined with bad temper, induces the husband to consult a specialist as to the sanity of his wife. When there is good ground for jealousy, the man threatens to kill the unfaithful wife; the woman her rival; thus both admitting that woman gives the first encouragement.

Quite a number of women bring false accusations against men of having taken liberties with them, and it is not always easy to prove that they suffer from hysteria. In some of these cases the "wish is father to the thought" or accusation. Auto-suggestion has a great deal to do with the immoral accusations of some women. Thus a girl was brought to me who complained that she could not go to public restaurants or tea-places without finding a man who attempted to assault her, at least she had that sensation.

As the flickering flame before it extinguishes will often burn up higher and brighter, so the sexual instinct in women at the change of life will show abnormal functioning before it is lost altogether. Many a woman at the "dangerous age" will do silly things, fall in love with a much younger man, who spurns her, and conduct herself in a manner that makes her the laughing-stock of her friends. Erotic delusions may occur. The revival of the passion may cause the wife to believe that she is neglected for some other woman, or a feeling of antipathy to her husband may arise which becomes misinterpreted for dislike on his part. During this stage of insane jealousy acts of violence and destructiveness are common. I have known many women at the climacteric develop most preposterous and obsessional notions as to gentlemen paying attention to them and proposing marriage. If such an idea remains a mere thought, kept to herself or merely communicated to her intimate friends, it is all very well; but I have known it to result in very unpleasant persecution of the supposed lovers and in most ludicrous acts with serious consequences. If there is any tendency to mental disorder, occult immoral influences may be believed to be exerted by the supposed lovers. Being a reputed hypnotist, I have had quite a number of women come to me with the request to dispel the evil influences of some man who was worrying them, especially at night. One admitted sending anonymous letters of a defamatory nature to a man, and assured me that such conduct was entirely against her character: "She must be hypnotised by him to do so. Could I break the spell?"

Middle-aged men are sometimes guilty of sexual offences. Their satiety breeds a demand for novelties. They are more or less impotent, and novelty alone serves to titillate their sexual brain centres. There is lack of self-control, and I have seen men of hitherto immaculate reputation become guilty of extraordinary conduct. Schoolmasters and clergymen who come in contact with little girls have consulted me from fear of giving way to their evil impulses; while others have come after being discovered to help them in case they get prosecuted. Occasionally other abnormal acts are indulged in, indecencies with little boys and exhibitionism, i.e. indecent exposure. In a number of these cases there is prostatic enlargement or disease, producing not only local irritation, but reflexly a constant psycho-sexual erethism. Relief of the prostatic difficulty often has a marvellous effect upon the morals of the subject.

In early locomotor ataxia and early general paralysis, lust is almost always present and commonly leads to adultery, but also to indecent assaults and improper exposure. Such patients have lost the sense of propriety and are apparently unconscious of doing wrong; at least they seem to take no precaution to prevent detection.

Precocity of the genital apparatus in boys is sometimes associated with defective secretion of the pineal gland and also with suprarenal tumours; and sexual infantilism with tumours of the pituitary body of the brain. I saw recently a girl, age nine years, sexually fully developed, looking fifteen or more, with big busts, broad hips, and hair on the pubes, who was mentally not older than four or five. She was a great trouble to her mother on account of the sexual advances she made to boys.

Satyriasis is a disease that occurs in the male; its principal manifestation is an abnormal excessive and unreasonable sexual desire. It is not frequently brought to the attention of the physician, save in the insane, probably because opportunities for gratification for the male are numerous. In my work *In Search of the Soul* I have produced a number of cases in which satyriasis was caused by injury to the back of the head.

Nymphomania is a disease analogous to satyriasis, occurring in the female. It is characterised by excessive and inordinate sexual desire, and often by the most pronounced lewdness and vulgarity. In severer forms it is likely to be associated with and dependent upon true insanity. In the work quoted I have given a number of cases due to brain disease. Inordinate sexual desire on the part of the female, falling short, perhaps, of true nymphomania, is not infrequent.

Sexual perversion may be defined, in a general way, as the possession of impulses to sexual gratification in an abnormal manner, with a partial or complete apathy towards the normal method. There is one element that predisposes to aberrations, namely, precocity. In early youth attraction towards the opposite sex is not yet distinct, and if the genetic instinct is nevertheless awakened, it may take a false path. Such uncertainty of the direction of erotic inclination makes it possible that the person who is precocious or ignorant may take to self-abuse, which is common both in the male and the female. Self-abuse is so common in early youth at puberty (I have seen a boy as young as four addicted to it), that, if kept within limits, it can hardly be described as perversion, for normal sexual intercourse is generally taken up in later years. The true perversion occurs only when a false orientation of the sexual function renders normal contact impossible, difficult, or repugnant, whilst it makes abnormal gratification easy, pleasing, or strongly desired.

As already mentioned, impotency, associated with desire, sometimes develops perversion. As a result, the deluded and unfortunate being seeks for new and varied means of sexual stimulation, often degrading in the extreme. There are numerous establishments in London, or at least there used to be, if the statements of my patients are to be trusted, whose principal business, although ostensibly for baths, massage, etc., is to cater to the perverted sexual tastes of a numerous class of patrons, especially elderly gentlemen. These establishments are principally for those with a predilection for abnormal methods of gratification with the opposite sex.

I will not enter here into the various methods of abnormal stimulation of the sexual organs. Only two methods that come within the province of the physician need be quoted here. The one is masochism, in which a person seeks and submits to pain, torture, and defilement, in order to stimulate and gratify his sexual instinct. It is a passive method. The other is an active and aggressive method, namely, sadism, in which the sexual instinct is stimulated and gratified by inflicting pain, cruelty or degradation on others. Usually sadism and masochism are found side by side in the same individual. The so-called lust murders are probably of this nature, strange mutilations and other performances being carried out in connection with the deed. Outrages on dead bodies and animals are generally committed by feeble-minded or insane individuals.

Sexual inversion or homosexuality, i.e. sexual predilection for the same sex, is frequent both in males and females. Homosexual tendencies appear sometimes in early youth and adolescence, but do not persist when rightly guided by experience and education in the widest sense of these words. In the majority of cases these manifestations must be attributed rather to a natural, unrecognised, undifferentiated, and unguided sexual instinct than to a naturally abnormal and necessarily perverted instinct. In a majority of such cases right guidance of these instincts, all too much neglected by those who have it in their power to give such guidance, would either prevent or readily correct such indulgences on the part of the young, who are really ignorant of the nature of the desires which move them. Companions in self-abuse are likely to turn homosexual. There is always a seducer and a misguided person. I once sat on the Bench next to a distinguished London magistrate, who sentenced heavily a number of young men who had been arrested by the police the day before, being discovered in a public convenience. I could not help expressing my surprise at the severity of the sentences, when my own observation of the accused persons led me to the conviction that the greater number of them were enticed to the place in ignorance and by curiosity, and should have had a chance of repentance without imprisonment, while the one or two actual culprits, who led these youths astray, should have received the most exemplary punishment.

True constitutional perversion is reached when the erring adolescent, instead of retracing his steps after the first occasion, continues in the way he has gone. Homosexuality in this conscious form, carried into overt action, is far more prevalent than is usually supposed. The magistrate to whom I have referred explained to me that he was so severe from a determination to stamp out the evil. Unfortunately, no punishment will do so.

There are two forms of homosexuality: the passive and the active form. The first is a developmental abnormality; the latter is acquired in the course of mental growth, and both forms must be considered as a neurosis. The passive or "subject homosexual," the true invert, feels like a woman and is attracted to mature, powerful men. He is an effeminate male, often of feminine features and feminine ways, and does not yield himself for gain or because of intimidation, but on account of spontaneous impulse, and joyfully. He is often mentally unbalanced or degenerate; and, if he practises his perverseness as a profession, he is simply a male prostitute and a potential, if not actual criminal. The active or "object homosexual" feels more like a man, and is attracted to boys and feminine men.

I have known some of these homosexuals to make ordinary marriages, either in the expectation that they would be able to reform, or in the hope of being able to hide their special weakness from the public, or with the object of having a family. Sometimes they succeed in their purpose, sometimes they fail; but pleasurable excitement is produced only rarely, and usually only by the necessary aid of the evocation of homosexual images.

Perverts, like normal lovers, often ignore the barriers that exist between the various social classes. Riches constitute an attraction to the poor invert, and poverty is an encouragement to the wealthy one, who sees his opportunity of bribing with money or dazzling with the prospect of luxury.

Unsuspecting parents are little aware how common homosexuality is among women, and how many little girls get seduced to the practice. The female Lesbian pervert may also be divided into two classes: the woman who seeks other women in order to carry out upon them male actions, and frequently delights in imitating male attire and male habits; and the passive woman who accepts the ardent caresses of other females. I have known a fashionable girls' school in London to be closed in consequence of the discovery of the degrading and criminal habits of the head-mistress who for years had seduced one girl after another.

If a homosexual male or female will volunteer to come for treatment, there is hope for them; but of the dozens that have consulted me only very few came a second time and kept up their attendance.

Fetishists are individuals whose amorous infatuations, instead of being aroused by an æsthetic criterion of the combined qualities of the opposite sex, are inspired only by an elementary and stereotyped impression, a single feature, which is always the same, a detached element, a single and relatively unimportant part of the body, devoid of any association either with the sexual act or with the real worth of the person loved on æsthetic grounds: the mouth, hands, feet, neck, hair, etc. Like sexual inversion, fetishism takes its origin in early adolescence from an erotic image, which presents itself perhaps by chance, and in virtue of priority acquires an enduring supremacy. Between this aphrodisiac image and sexual excitement there is established an obligatory connection, a sort of mental ankylosis, a necessary relation that excludes every other relation.

Another abnormality of the sex instinct consists in the tendency to gaze and peep at objects of sexual interest, the victims being generally known as "voyeurs," a practice for which Paris is said to afford special facilities.

Still another abnormality exists in these persons who, as already mentioned, find pleasure in exposing their sexual organs. Such are known as the "exhibitionists." The two are often combined in the same individual.

What parents and teachers should do by way of sex education is a big subject, which would fill a separate volume. So far as the medical psychologist is concerned, I can only repeat that those who have been seduced to perverse habits, but recognise the error of their ways, can be reformed by individual psychotherapy. The professionals do not consult a physician.

Freud claims that the sex instinct in an obscure form and not related to the function of reproduction exists already in the infant, and enables it to secure various forms of pleasurable sensations, such as the auto-excitation of certain particularly sensitive parts of the body, the so-called "eroto-genetic zones." In his view, the child has in him the germs of all the forms of perversion met with in the adult, and in spite of his "angel mien" is really a "polymorph pervert." About the third or fourth year, however, the whole of this infantile sexuality becomes repressed by education and by the development of feelings of shame, loathing, disgust, and morality. From the fifth or sixth year onwards the child strives to come into closer relationship with the outside world, and seeks to love somebody other than itself; the boy generally his mother or nurse, the girl her father. This gives rise to sexual phantasies referring to the parents, which may be completely forgotten in later life, but still exert an unconscious influence. As an explanation of sexual perversion the individual is imagined to have stopped short in one of the early stages. But neurasthenia, hysteria, and insanity also are claimed to be caused by the enforced repression of the sexual complexes. To bring these by the methods of psychoanalysis into light of day in all their nakedness and ugliness is sufficient to deprive them of their noxious virtue, and to restore to the patient mental and physical health.

CHAPTER IX

THE EGOTIST, AUTOCRAT, AND THE DOMINEERING MAN

SELF-PRESERVATION is opposed by the gregarious instinct. Primitive man, unprotected against the forces of nature and at the mercy of every foe, found it of advantage to cultivate the society of his fellows. He found that living in numbers rendered him more powerful and enabled him to give effect to the advantage of his superior intelligence. Specialisation of employment became possible in social life. Grouping among men was all the more necessary because of the long protection needed by their offspring. The long association before children became independent gave rise to an attachment between child and child, and child and parent, between brothers and sisters, friend and friend, and so on, thus forming the foundation of social life. Again, family life awakened in primitive man feelings of love and tenderness for those who excited in him no fear of rivalry. Gradually these sympathies widened till they embraced the tribe and ultimately the whole human race.

The possession of the gregarious instinct, even in great strength, does not necessarily imply sociability of temperament. Many a man in a big city leads a most solitary, unsociable life who yet would find it hard to live far away from the crowd. Such men are unsociable but gregarious; and they illustrate the fact that sociability, although it has the gregarious instinct as its foundation, is a more complex, more highly developed tendency.

Social attachment necessitates renunciation. To share the advantages, the protection, of the community, we must abandon the freedom allowable to a solitary man and restrain ourselves in every direction. Those who lack this sentiment are likely to sacrifice friends if their interests should suffer. To a certain extent the foundation of all morality is domestic; for even now parental and conjugal sympathies, as they were the first to appear, so are they still the most fundamental. When a man has run his mortal race, if for his epitaph we may truly write that he was an affectionate man, a kind husband, and a tender father, we imply a character of fundamental goodness from which other moral qualities may be inferred. If we can add that he was a true friend and a devoted citizen, in that collection of parental, conjugal, and social sympathies we describe the full measure of ordinary practical activity.

In every community, conformity, not only of conduct, but of opinion, of each, with the conduct and opinion of the rest, is regarded with approval;

and conduct and opinion that do not conform to the common standard meet with strong reprobation, and sometimes with vigorous suppression. Consequently we find strongly implanted among the dispositions of every member of the community the " desire to conform," to do as others do, to fall in with the prevailing mode of action. The good citizen is he who is satisfied with existing conditions and is obedient to authority. Conformity to the customs of the community is usually regarded as morality ; but true morality is to do what we believe to be right, merely because it is right. We should disapprove of ourselves if we acted otherwise, and our own disapproval is more than we can bear ; so we do what we believe to be right, even though, in so doing, we incur the disapproval of others. This conflict produces the " conscientious objector."

Many people do not act on the motive of securing their own approval, but accept the conventional morality they find prevalent. They are actuated by the " desire to please," to earn the approval of those who are dear to them and with whom they live in companionship. A man must so order his conduct as to gain the approval and good opinion of those with whom he consorts, and the desire of gaining and retaining this good opinion is one of the strongest of the motives by which his conduct is prompted and regulated. Such is the origin of love of praise and dread of blame, which are necessary elements in social life and give rise to the desire to excel ; that is, to ambition. Duties are enjoined on the young by parents and elders ; and certain acts are forbidden or punished, others are applauded or rewarded. The public opinion of society carries on the process.

Love of approbation causes men in their social intercourse to be courteous, conciliatory, and polite. It gives rise to display ; thus refinement is promoted and people become mindful of appearances. In excess it causes people to seek popularity though destitute of talents ; and, when deficient, the person does not care whether he pleases or displeases, and, though he may be possessed of talents, he may lack the ambition to exert them.

The reward of applause and the punishment of reprobation are a guide to conduct, and with many constitute a sense of duty. But this often leads to imitations of the general example and therefore does not deserve our approval, as when a person who has really little or no religious feelings is a regular church-goer, simply because he is afraid of his neighbours ; or, the man who is a Tory or Liberal in politics because the one or the other party-view appears to be held by the majority ; or again, the person who subscribes to a charity not from a benevolent disposition, but because his neighbour has done the same. Such actions are not dictated by a desire to do good to humanity, but are stimulated merely by a desire to obtain the applause of mankind. In obedience to the promptings of this faculty men will erect hospitals, endow universities, provide homes for the destitute. Many of our most noble institutions would fall into insolvency if all the contributions to their funds which did not arise from a pure motive of benevolence were withdrawn. Benevolence alone would never do the noble deeds that the desire to please, to gain esteem, and to become notorious does.

From the desire to earn the admiration of one's fellow-men arose ambition, which we may define as that anxious aspiration, so characteristic of the human species, to rise above our respective stations, or to attain to something loftier and, as fancy pictures, better than we now enjoy. Ambition is one of the qualities necessary to industry. It is the greatest motive power to achievement. But ambition in young people must not be mistaken for capacity; otherwise disappointment will follow, and the father who, for example, entertains a vague and complacent conviction that he is rearing an Archbishop, or a Lord Chancellor, or a great author, may have to be exceedingly pleased ten years later to learn that his lad evinces a genius for book-keeping by double entry and for mounting a high stool with punctuality.

There are persons with inordinate ambition, and appetite for honours which can never be satisfied; feeding only serves to aggravate its hunger. No sooner has the ambitious man gained one eminence than another and yet loftier aim becomes visible, and with fresh and more eager efforts and desires he strains forward to reach the summit. Ambition has two sources: the love of reputation and the love of power. Whereas love of approbation confines itself to a narrow circle, love of reputation embraces a wider one. If love of reputation includes a wide area and is for a long period of time, it is called love of fame. If the desire is merely to be talked about, it is love of notoriety. Men may commit all sorts of actions to achieve that end. People with a disposition to plume themselves on any petty, accidental, or temporary cause of superiority to their fellow-men are called vain. If the fear of disapprobation leads to confusion, we call it shame. It occurs on being discovered, but may be prospective and prevent us from doing things which are condemned by our friends or by public opinion.

Ambition is a complex attribute which may be stimulated by cupidity or avarice, love of power, love of family, or a desire to excel, animated on the one hand by sheer egotism, or on the other by a desire to develop one's self to the limit of one's capacity as a personal and social duty. The dread of poverty and a desire for independence are among the stimuli which, singly or combined, develop it. Even so laudable an ambition as that inspired by a desire to provide luxuries for one's family may be a feeder for crime, where the moral equilibrium of the ambition-driven subject is defective. Ambition fed by sexual love has filled many a convict cell. Ambition and discontent are twin qualities of the mind. The discontent of humanity is the seed from which civilisation has sprung.

Ambition, whether for good or bad, needs a forceful character. Many a criminal and colossal swindler placed in the right position for the legitimate exercise of his faculties might have earned the esteem of mankind. An earnest and vigorous character infused with the passion of ambition is bound to be self-assertive, strenuous, exercising his tendency openly and rudely or secretly and subtly, for his natural impulse is to appropriate to himself what can be useful, either as conqueror or criminal, saint or sinner, according to circumstances. He must suffer and do many unworthy things that are hurtful to character, for he must reckon with the meanness, the guile, the intrigues, the interests of those with whom and against whom it is necessary to act. The fine-textured, tender, and scrupulous nature which cannot bargain with and manage that which revolts its sensibilities as wrong, mean, or unclean, is not practical enough to succeed well; it would have the ideal to be the real, which is madness, and things behind the scenes to look as they do on the stage, which is absurd. If it be pain and grief to anyone to hurt another by pushing before him, there is an end of ambition; for, as Seneca said, ambition looks not backwards at those whom it has beaten, it suffers by seeing a single person before it on the track of its goal. Withal, its very nature is still to rise, for its horizon ever widens as it mounts. To count ambition a vice would be to imply that man had risen to his present plane of being by means of his vices.

The social life led some men to comport themselves according to the ideas of others, but some became distinguished by preferring to act in accordance with their own views. They were men who set more value on their own opinions than on those of others. This gave them self-reliance and independence of character, self-confidence and self-satisfaction, which enabled their mental powers to act to the best advantage. These were the born commanders. The man who desires to command and rule is necessary to all organisation, political, military, or industrial. Just as the man who loves approbation is desirous of fame, so the man with large self-esteem loves power. The direction the love of fame or power will take is determined by the strength of the other faculties. Thus wealth, political or military fame, or even mere brute strength—in short, almost anything that can distinguish us from the crowd—may under different influences become the object of our aspirations. The method employed to gratify our ambitions depends also on the strength of the other faculties. Some will employ honest, others more or less dishonest, open or secretive methods.

Self-assurance is a very useful attribute. It is helpful in every walk of life. The self-confident man steps to the front while his brother, much more highly gifted, perhaps, but lacking his self-assurance, is left behind. Who does not know of men who achieved success through sheer "cheek," and of others whose reserve and diffidence have prevented them from attaining the position to which their abilities entitled them? Doubtless the success of the self-assured man is largely the outcome of the sense of well-being and exuberant energy accompanying it. The energy impels a man to be up and doing, while the self-confidence gives promise of victory. A person who is too sensitive and lacks self-assurance will never do, for example, for a commercial traveller. If he is kicked out by one door, he must have the courage to re-enter by another. The man who is too sensitive will shun that merchant ever after. Psychologists who give advice on the selection of vocations should take note of this. Self-esteem and self-satisfaction become morbid and greatly exaggerated in the early stages of certain mental disorders; and they become diminished to a feeling of absolute unworthiness in other forms of mental disorder.

The civilisation of every country depends upon a small number of eminent men; therefore the rest of us must have instincts and dispositions impelling us to follow leaders: such as suggestibility, imitation, veneration, etc. The self-reliant man is well satisfied with himself no matter what his intellect, personal talents, birth, or fortune; he does not envy a king. On the other hand, those deficient in this respect will be remarkable for their humility. It is a wise provision of nature that persons in the meanest situations and with the humblest acquirements have a sense of self-importance. It renders its possessors happy and contented with that "modicum of sense" which has been conferred upon them, who otherwise would be miserable if aware of their deficiencies.

We talk a great deal of liberty, forgetting the fact that obedience gives restful happiness to millions of mankind. Many a slave has been freed who would have preferred to remain with his old master. Love of liberty may be regarded as the counterpart of the love of power. As the superior desires power, so the inferior desires liberty; that is to say, emancipation from the power of his superior. Where the power of which the exertion is resented is moral and not physical, the appropriate phrase is not love of liberty, but love of independence.

Self-esteem in excess leads to conceit and arrogance Self-esteem is often exaggerated to the ridiculous, sometimes with reference to personal attractiveness, sometimes in regard to intellectual ability. The "bore" has plenty of it. Where our regard for self keeps us from performing certain actions deemed unworthy of ourselves, we call the attitude self-respect. But what we consider unworthy is, for most of us, determined by what our social environment considers to be unworthy. What is ordinarily called self-respect really is dependent, in the great majority of cases, on what people generally think regarding such matters.

Self-esteem and love of approbation are often confounded. By the one sentiment a man esteems himself ; by the other he courts the esteem of others. They are best distinguished by their abuse. The one is pride, the other vanity ; the one assumes, the other begs ; hence it is truly remarked that an individual is too proud to be vain. Pride is more connected with command, and vanity with taking counsel. The vain man attaches the utmost importance to the opinions entertained of him by others, and seeks with eagerness to gain their approbation ; the proud man expects mankind will come to him and acknowledge his merit. The vain man knocks at every door to draw attention towards himself, and supplicates the smallest position of honour ; the proud man despises these marks of distinction, which on the vain confer the most perfect delight. The proud man is disgusted by indiscreet eulogisms ; the vain man inhales with ecstasy the incense of flattery, although profusely offered and by no very skilful hand. Yet great self-esteem, if not actual conceit, is consistent with a sensitive regard for the opinions of others. It is quite possible for a person to hold himself in high esteem and yet live in fear that others may not take him at his own valuation.

Persons with large self-esteem have confidence in their own powers, value their own judgment, and are willing to assume responsibility. If intellectually gifted, they may undervalue the talents of others ; and with small intellect there may be a conceit of abilities not possessed. When there is little self-esteem, a person gives in to the judgment of others easily, lacks independence, self-confidence, natural dignity, self-reliance. And if given to respect authority as well, he is liable to under-rate his own abilities, and more apt to follow than to lead. Little self-esteem in a cautious person is likely to make him afraid to exert himself; but, gifted intellectually, he may lead off well when once placed in a responsible position, though at first he distrusts his own capabilities.

Self-reliance imparts a resolute character, not easily influenced by others: the helpless man lacks constancy, for his actions depend on the influence of others; his conduct is therefore not uniform. Belief in one's own powers gives tenacity of purpose and firmness; if in excess, stubbornness and obstinacy. Some persons yield readily; it may be said of some they scarcely have a will of their own; they follow the last impulse they receive, and, without strength to resist, they are easy instruments of all whom they meet. They give up persevering under difficulties; they decline to follow the estimable motto, "Try again." Others are of an immovable character, firm in their resolutions and constant in their principles; they do not attend to exhortations or to examples; their conduct is uniform, and their exertions may be calculated on in the various situations of life.

Stability of character is often called strength of will. A man who adheres tenaciously to his resolutions is called a strong-willed man, and, if this tendency exists in excess, an obstinate man. On the other hand, a man who vacillates, or frequently changes his resolutions, is called a man of weak will. Such a man is too easily influenced for the bad, and in any case fit only for an employee. The strong-willed person refuses to be the sport of circumstances, to drift with the current, but strikes boldly out for some definite point on life's shore. Such will-power and tenaciousness will be found in most cases to be hereditary, and as regards its scope and direction only shall we find it the sport of circumstances. Small minds often exhibit a tenaciousness that leads them to success, for they are capable of being entirely directed by one unchanging motive. Larger minds often fail of success by reason of consistency in pursuit due to the varied play of many motives, each capable of strong attraction, on a richly endowed nature. It is the person who has definite aims in life who will appear to possess the strongest will. The habit of perseverance or of continuous effort is that which, added to energy, constitutes industry. Patience is passive endurance of labour, but also endurance under fatigue and suffering in general.

CHAPTER X

THE MORALLY WEAK-MINDED

THE wish to live in families imposed upon man certain obligations and duties which varied according to the wants and habits of each community. Man had to act not solely for his own benefit but had to take the welfare of his family or community into consideration. Moral conduct became essentially social conduct—conduct conducive to the well-being and progress of the race—at all events the higher forms of it, which involve the voluntary control and regulation of the instinctive impulses. Such conduct is disapproved of which, if freely indulged in, would lead to the degeneration if not extinction of mankind. Morality thus simply includes the rules and regulations by which we may all live together in the happiest manner possible. The great principle has always been: Do unto others as you would be done by; or the negative: Do not to others what you would not wish that they should do to you.

The sentiments of common interests in the primitive family and tribe and the habitual reprobation of certain acts by individuals as injurious to the family or tribe, in course of time generated a sentiment of right and wrong in regard to such acts; but the approbation or disapprobation, which may turn our choice, may not be of our fellows, but of ourselves. In fact, man, in the solitude of his own thoughts is still a social animal, and creates a companion out of himself—a critic to whose praise and blame he is keenly sensitive. When a man does or refrains from doing an action which he thinks is right or wrong, he is guided in his conduct by the application of certain rules or principles implanted in his mind, either naturally or by the influence of external circumstances. When this moral judgment becomes so active in its operation as to be instinctive, it is called conscience.

Whenever a man does anything which he knows would meet with the disapprobation of his friends, he experiences a feeling of uneasiness, a feeling of guilt; and when he does something which would be applauded by his fellows, he has a sense of happiness. But this desire of approbation is not the only factor in moral conduct. With many, if not most, men, the practice of morality extends only so far as they think they can perceive some personal advantage and immunity of punishment. Hence it is that those who can extensively foresee future consequences of their acts are more moral than those who are ignorant; not so much because they have better intentions as because they can perceive the future effects more clearly than those whose minds are more occupied by immediate pleasure and personal desires.

The so-called moral sense is not a simple activity, but the sum of a set of tendencies; originating in the social sentiments largely guided by the approbation of our fellow-men, ruled by reason, self-interest, religious feeling, and experience of the more remote consequences of our actions. Therefore the character of moral deficiency may vary very widely in different cases, according as one or other of the constituent elements is lacking or is imperfectly developed. Training and circumstances add further to the variety. That this moral sense, this approbation of self, this conscience, is not the product of a purely reflective faculty we see in children from the earliest age. Some have it strongly without teaching or example; others have it sparingly, and need the most assiduous care to develop it. It is by no means exceptional to find persons of normal and even acute intelligence who appear to have little or no moral feeling. Their sublimation and rationalisation hides their criminal tendencies. Indeed, a lack of ethical feeling is often an advantage. Some of our most successful public men would not be in the positions they now occupy if they were too tender-hearted. On the other hand, a lack of intellect is always a drawback.

The dishonest man need not necessarily be dishonest in all things. He may show great honesty in most affairs. Nor is there here included the class of offenders who transgress only when they are out of work during certain seasons of the year. I remember one young woman whom I came across in my young days who was respectably employed but appeared to me to have a type of head which I, from my visits to prisons both here and on the Continent, learned to associate with thieving tendencies. I knew every such type does not necessarily take to thieving, so I put the question as delicately as I could whether she did not sometimes feel strange impulses to abstract things that did not belong to her. To my great delight she replied: "Only when I am hard up."

By some, moral transgression is attributed entirely to impairment of will, as if man were instinctively moral in tendency and, when he does not follow his moral impulse, simply lacks the will to follow them. This is a mistake. There is at first in all of us a constant conflict between the moral, i.e. the altruistic sentiments and the self-preserving tendencies, though some are by nature endowed more with the one than the other. When we say that a man with a relatively weak will is more liable to transgressions, we really want to indicate that there is such a lack of balance in the arrangement and degree of the various mental powers that he is the play of circumstances and can be easily influenced in one or other direction. The man with selfish instincts in predominance will exercise his will in that direction, and will have a powerful volition towards moral obliquity; just as another man possessed by altruistic sentiments may have an equally strong will not to commit breaches of social ethics without any effort of self-control whatever. Children are relatively strong-willed, yet still defective in moral sense and conscience, their altruistic sentiments being still latent.

All the moral dispositions require education: a love of justice, even if innate, does not tell us what is just. The selfish tendencies, on the other hand, manifest themselves without training and spontaneously, and are therefore more active in the child, which has yet to learn self-control before the moral sentiments can manifest themselves. Nearly all moral disease arises from unregulated desire. Every desire exposes a man to the temptation of gratifying it, and animal desires are usually the most imperative.

The exercise of self-restraint to prevent injuring others in person, or property, or feeling, constitutes morality; and the doing of such injurious acts is immorality, and may or may not be crime, according as it is or is not punishable by law. Immorality and crime, then, are disorders of conduct in the sense that they are departures from what the universal consent of mankind admits that conduct ought to be. The man in whom the altruistic sentiments are stronger than the egoistic propensities will be good by nature; the man likely to sin is the man in whom the altruistic and selfish tendencies are equally balanced and who is therefore more at the mercy of external circumstances. Then there are men who simply follow their animal inclinations, lacking in their organisation any checking power of social or altruistic feeling. These are the morally weak-minded.

Scratch ever so lightly the back of civilised man—remove his inhibitions, as by a blow on the head which obliterates all his higher attributes—and we find the animal nature, i.e. the primary instincts. As a rule, the higher mental powers, those which are added latest in the scale of evolution, are the first to deteriorate in anything that affects the brain, whether by poisons, injury, or disease; hence a change in the moral nature of man is often the first symptom of unsoundness of mind. The person becomes abnormally egoistic, or else there is apathy and indifference, or complete ethical insensibility.

The moral character evolves slowly in childhood, is at its best throughout middle age, and undergoes frequently remarkable transformations in the involution process of old age. There are men who, as they grow old, lose all feelings of affection, take a dislike to their own children, and exercise a headstrong tyranny over those who are dependent upon them; or they become erotic, vain, ambitious, or utterly selfish. Others become more indulgent, amiable, generous and more serene than they used to be, owing to the disappearance of disturbing passions and pre-occupations. There are some who lose in virtue and there are others who lose some faults.

Cleverness in planning crimes does not exclude weak-mindedness. It is simply the employment of what intellect there is available for the purpose of gratifying a passion. Even idiots confined in institutions sometimes show cleverness in the mischief they do. Strong propensities, in man as in animals, give inventiveness and craftiness in the employment of means to gratify a desire. This would explain the apparent contradiction in the intellectual manifestations of a criminal who from one point of view appears almost a genius and from another mentally deficient. Lack of intelligence impairs the capacity to appreciate the nature and consequences of conduct, and reduces the inhibitory control over the propensities, thus leading to acts of impulse. Stealing and sexual offences are common; but if very deficient, such persons may also commit crimes of arson, sometimes apparently from no other motive than the desire to see a blaze; and they may make murderous assaults under trivial provocation owing to an inability to appreciate the nature and effect of what they are doing.

The weak-minded criminals commonly are habitual criminals, men who live by dishonest means owing to defective mental constitution. Punishment has little effect on them, and they do not fear going to prison. They are mental defectives, not genuine criminals. They cannot " will " an honest life. To this class belong the foolish odds and ends of humanity, the people of no foresight. No doubt there are among them some who are gifted with exceptional capacity, but even with these there is a weak point in the moral harness. A great character sets his face like a flint against the seduction which, if yielded to, would prove his undoing; but, where the character is weak, temptation is succumbed to with fatal facility, and in due course the weakling swells the ranks of the criminal classes.

That a large number of criminals have not the same vitality and intelligence as law-abiding citizens is shown conclusively by the following observations: The mortality among juveniles in reformatory schools is higher than the mortality among the general population of a similar age. It has also been pointed out that the juvenile prison population, as a whole, is under the average weight of the general community at the same period of life. Further, it has been shown that a high percentage of these juveniles are descended from such a feeble stock that over 30 per cent. of the industrial school, reformatory school, and prison population have lost one or both parents in early life. In other words, the physical basis of mental life is in a worse condition amongst juvenile offenders as a body than amongst the ordinary population at the same stage of existence. In addition, it has been shown that nearly one-third of the inmates of reformatories descended on one or both sides from parents who neglected to control them, or deserted them, or were in prison for crime. The majority are either unable to read and write, or can read or write only imperfectly, many because of defective mental capacity. Owing to their inherited incapacities and to certain surroundings, a large number of mental defectives tend to become criminals; and a considerable proportion of so-called criminals or law-breakers are demonstrably mentally defective.

Reading the police reports one is struck by the number of apparently purposeless crimes that are committed. It is not to be wondered at when we realise how large is the proportion of the weak-minded. As the lame man wants his physical crutch, so these poor creatures need their mental crutch, and when that is withdrawn many of them inevitably fall. The more amenable they have been to good influences, the more readily may they succumb to bad ones. They lack will-power, and this must be superimposed from without. If it be a power for good, all is well; if for evil, as it generally is, the result is disastrous. Criminals, paupers, drunkards, prostitutes have frequently descended to these conditions because they are feeble-minded, and our charitable and State institutions, homes, industrial schools, reformatories and prisons fail to stem the evils with which they contend, because the public acts on the assumption that temporary care and training are all that are needed. It is sad to remember how many charitable agencies are wasting their powers, because they do not understand that it is impossible to rescue the weak-minded unless it is done once for all. People who deal with these degenerates and see them under control, behaving in decent and orderly fashion and generally maintaining good habits, are apt to forget that the control, and that alone, is the cause of the good behaviour, that as soon as this control is removed these weak-minded men and women are likely to succumb to any other influence which may be brought to bear.

We have already pointed out that it is the highly developed intellect of man which changes the innate animal propensities into glorious faculties. Thus the animal desire of propagating the species is transformed in man to moral love; the love of female animals for their offspring, provided by nature to preserve their young, becomes in women the amiable virtue which inspires their tenderness for their children; the attachment of animals changes in man to friendship; their sensibility to caresses changes into ambition and a sentiment of honour; the instinctive building of nests by birds and of huts by beavers is at the root of man's nobler dwellings, of his temples and palaces. From this one might wrongly conclude that the development of the moral sense is in proportion to the development of the intellect. But this is not so, for, as everyone knows, there are moral idiots as well as intellectual idiots—men born with fair intellect but with an entire absence of the higher moral sentiments, entirely destitute of moral feeling. They are as insensible to the moral relations of life, as deficient in this regard as a person colour-blind is to certain colours, or as one without ear for music is to the finest harmonies of sound. If caught in an immoral or criminal act, they show no repentance. They may perhaps feel and dread the material consequences of crime, but they are deficient in the feeling of moral guilt. They are not lacking in intelligence; but their instincts are put to bad use.

The cases of moral weak-mindedness that come before the physician are usually young people, of respectable family, clever but conspicuously lacking in wisdom and discretion and destitute of feeling for social obligations. Many of them evince from early childhood lack of affection, dishonesty, callousness, utter indifference to the welfare and feelings of those around them, unkind to their brothers and sisters and to animals, fond of practical jokes, irritable and hasty in temper, rebellious to authority, sulky when corrected, and sullen and morose. Punishment arouses in them only a sense of injustice, of injured innocence, and of rankling vindictiveness. As they get older they may be addicted to petty thefts, which are often concealed with an amount of cunning that would hardly be credited by those who have no experience in these cases. They do not appreciate the enormity of their offence, and when found out they exhibit no sense of shame. When they are punished and express regret, it is forgotten when the next temptation comes. They are unmanageable at school and are a danger to other children. If they can get through their school and college career by their cleverness and quick understanding—never by industry—and have avoided expulsion for their conduct, they still fail in life, for they live from hand to mouth.

Many of the cases that have come before me were well-educated young men and women, plausible talkers, of prepossessing appearance, but decidedly cunning. Their chief characteristic was inveterate lying. Such people fabricate stories to obtain what they desire, and their chief offence is usually having obtained money or credit by false pretences. If we go carefully through the history of the patients, we find that from early childhood there existed an incapacity to tell the truth. These children lie to themselves and to others continually, until they are no longer capable of distinguishing clearly between that which has been experienced and that which has been invented. This habit, unless treated early, becomes rooted and remains through life. In adult years such persons cheat and make up things, either half-consciously or quite unconsciously. They are instinctive liars and are incapable of speaking the truth, even if they are put on their oath. The pathological liar confuses the products of his fancy with realities. False memories constantly disturb his reproductive faculty. Since he plunges with his whole attention into the deceptive creations of his fancy, in such a way that they become realities to him, he has an assured appearance, and he presents his humbugs and swindles so ingeniously and naturally, with such an innocent expression or with such unfeigned enthusiasm, that he succeeds again and again in convincing his fellow-men, where a conscious liar, who coolly and clearly measures his words in constant fear of contradicting himself or being trapped, meets with instinctive mistrust. In the consciousness of the common or normal liar two trains of thought flow beside each other—the thought of the truth and the thought of the lie—and they trip each other up. In the brain of the pathological liar all is unified, and so he can carry through the most magnificent swindles artistically and with inner conviction. Thus he drags a multitude of credulous souls with him to ruin. The public believe blindly in his alluring portrayals, his poetic effusions, his fairy-tales, until at last some chance, or the reflection of a thoughtful man, brings the end with panic, and usually a sensation in the courts. Then, as though wakening from a dream, the pathological liar collapses, for the moment almost as astonished and dismayed as his victim—only to begin soon again, for he cannot help himself.

Such people cannot meet life's problems squarely, but resort to fantastic means. They are inexhaustible talkers, given to romancing, and transforming simple daily events into extraordinary experiences, in order to make themselves interesting. I hold the records of more than one woman who played in succession the rôle of a peeress, poor student, rich friend of a bishop or nobleman, charity organiser, estate owner, discarded wife of a Cabinet Minister, and so on. As a rule their lying is a mixture of imagination, boastfulness, deception, delusion and dissimulation. The possibility that the untruth may be at any minute demolished does not abash these liars in the least. Remonstrances against the lies make no impression, for their lies are real experiences to them, and they can glory in them, and recount their fabrications with an infinity of detail. I examined a boy, during the war, who had run away from home when threatened with castigation for one of his many misdeeds. Though captured by the police and returned home, where he was practically kept locked up until he appeared before the magistrate, he nevertheless had the audacity to tell me he had been up in an observation balloon the night before and watched a Zeppelin raid, of which he gave such a perfect and interesting description, probably a combination of what he had read before and his own romantic fancy, that any newspaper editor might have been glad of the account. With many of these youths there is combined with this love of romancing a love of adventure. A large number do run away, and that repeatedly; others, forced to stay at home and seeing no chance of escape, content themselves with inventing stories of escapades.

The mistake is often made of regarding these offenders, because they can talk well, as mentally normal; but brilliant conversational powers are not incompatible with mental aberrations, including well-defined insanity, such as hypomania. In every lunatic asylum there are harmless patients who are entertaining, humorous and witty, and would talk inexhaustibly if they could find people to listen to them. It is on account of their pretty high level of intelligence that the offences of the morally weak-minded consist mostly of swindling. They are exercising a talent, and not, like the ordinary swindler, following a trade. They will lie and cheat even when there is no prospect of gain and a certainty of detection, and persist in their perverted conduct in the absence of intelligent motive.

Next to their lack of industry and chronic mendacity, their most conspicuous quality is an absence of all compassion. The misery they cause to their parents and shame to their friends is nothing to them; and, worse still, I have seen a good many wicked enough either to plan or to permit suspicion or blame to fall upon others, and in one case, as I have already mentioned, to allow the wrongly accused and found guilty to go to prison. Their most marked characteristic is a lack of power to recognise ethical distinctions, a lack of conscience of the sense of right and duty; and through this moral deprivation there is a serious lack of balance between the thinking and acting capacities. Without this power there is no check to the lower passions except by the intellectual consideration of utility and expediency, and unbridled egoism has full play. In the milder cases the individual may merely be exceptionally self-centred, incapable of appreciating the rights and feelings of others, and governing his conduct entirely by his own likes and dislikes, to which everything has to give way.

Another manifestation of their intense egotism is their entire lack of appreciation of kindness done them or benefits of which they have been the recipients. They are ungrateful and abusive to those who have served them. At the same time, if advantages are yet to be gained, they are sycophantic to nauseousness in their deportment towards those from whom the favours are to come. It is held by some that the morally weak-minded lack wisdom, failing to see that they will be detected; but with this view I cannot agree, for I have found that such people often escape and reckon upon it, as far as they reckon upon anything; and actually only a small portion of their misdeeds is ever brought home to them. They may talk morals, but they are not moral, although they often buy things for others with the proceeds of their frauds and thefts. Regular life is too monotonous for them. They are not made for steady industry. They trade upon the credulity and ignorance of good people.

I have known a man urging at a medical meeting stricter tests of examination, when he himself had forged a medical diploma and was practising as an aural specialist, having acquired apparently sufficient knowledge by attending post-graduate instruction. He even published a medical work, and the errors contained therein first aroused my suspicion. Just then he was arrested for another big fraud combined with forgery and brought before the criminal courts; but the fact that he posed as a qualified physician was suppressed, probably to save the reputation of the many friends he had gained in the profession. As far as appearances went he appeared an honourable man, and I knew him as an excellent husband and fond father.

Whereas according to the theory I have formulated there are definite regions in the brain for the primary emotions and instinctive impulses, injury of which is liable to cause exaggerated manifestation of the particular activity with which it is connected, I have found no such region connected with the moral sentiment. In all the clinical literature of head-injuries there is not a case in which the moral sentiment alone was lost or exaggerated. And this harmonises with the psychological view that the moral sentiment is a complex faculty, a balancing between different motives, requiring more or less judgment. It is therefore not surprising that injury of the frontal lobes of the brain, which have to do with the intellectual functions, leading to some destruction of that area, should weaken inhibition and consequently cause greater activity of the animal instincts; at least in those in whom they were strong before the accident, but kept under control, which has now been destroyed. I have given numerous cases in my work *In Search of the Soul* of frontal injury followed by moral changes; and in some, where surgical treatment was undertaken, recovery followed.

For the more serious cases of moral weak-mindedness, chronic from infancy, there is little hope. Education cannot eradicate what is bred in the organisation. For them segregation in institutions, though a hardship, is the best for them and for the community. At present they receive ever-increasing sentences of imprisonment, which have no effect whatever on them. For the milder cases where there is some rudiment of affection, of conscience, or honest ambition, there is hope under appropriate treatment. Together with other measures, psychotherapy holds out the best promise. Several of my cases thus treated have reached even distinction in due course, when employment was found for them where their talents, hitherto wasted in a mischievous manner for ill-deeds, had a proper field for exercise.

"Moral weak-mindedness" is legally recognised up to the age of sixteen under the Mental Deficiency Act of 1913. Over that age the morally deficient must take the consequences of their acts according to the nature of their crimes.

CHAPTER XI

MORAL RESPONSIBILITY

WE have shown that man's personality is a federation of organic impulses, arising from hereditary tendencies and acquired habits. Man shares with animals certain instincts which urge for gratification. They are his driving forces to action. They are kept in check in the first instance by their own antagonism, as, for example, at the sight of danger, when two impulses may arise simultaneously—to fight and to run away. But otherwise before the organisation of social life, man did not feel that he had any duties except towards himself. When another animal or one of his fellows opposed him in the immediate realisation of some appetite or some desire, his only idea was to suppress that obstacle, and he disposed of the adversary by a quick and violent movement, not moderated by anything, unless it were the recollection of a former defeat. When he was victorious, when the possession of some rich spoil had rewarded his actions, we may be sure that he knew neither sorrow nor remorse, but merely pleasure in gratification and pride in his strength.

Not only the conflict of the primary instincts with one another, but especially the conflict of the herd instinct with the egoistic instincts, limited the possibility of impulsive action. As social life progressed so affection increased for parents, wife, children, friends and acquaintances, desires for their love and esteem arose, and ambition to rise in the social circle and community. These feelings and desires produced further conflict with the selfish impulses and tended to check action which would make void the comforts and advantages of social regard. As tribal religion and government came into being there arose in addition veneration for authority, for established institutions, for antiquated rites and ceremonies, and this tended further to the suppression of selfishness and the submission to established order. Social life further generated compassion and benevolence towards the helpless, and developed the original instincts of imitation and the tendency to suggestibility.

Man has therefore a large variety of motives, and according to the measure of his intelligence he can weigh them, estimate possible consequences, and follow one and inhibit the others. The better furnished his intellect, the greater the check on his actions. The primary instincts, such as cupidity, sexuality, the instinct of destruction, may want to be satisfied; but the man's intelligence shows him that the result of such satisfaction will be to harm him in his property, liberty, in his life, for the injustice and injury he is doing to others, and thus his instincts are regulated. It is not the intellect, then, that drives to action, but the inherent instinctive motives which determine conduct. The intellect can choose when there is more than one motive; but it may also be employed for the gratification of one solitary desire. Peaceful social life, constant employment and adequate means for the sustenance of life, save man more and more from the exercise of his lower instincts, and with leisure he is able to direct them into more refined and useful channels.

All the primary instincts are unconscious; that is to say, we are not aware of them until the impulse has arisen and has given rise to an idea or has been spontaneously translated into action. The intellect steps in afterwards to discover the reason for our conduct. Were there only selfish propensities, all our actions might be automatic, reflex, unconscious; but their own antagonism and their antagonism to the higher impulses springing from social life, as well as the acquired stock of ideas and habits of conduct impressed upon us by our environment from childhood onwards, produce conflicts which rise into consciousness, and enable us to exercise choice according to the degree of strength of the various dispositions. As a rule we follow the strongest impulse, but we can go contrary to it, owing to the moral habits we have acquired in the course of our lives or by reflection on the possible consequences. Just as the conceited man has acquired that character by habit and manifests it now unconsciously, but is able to change by consciously directing his attention to his peculiarity, so, for example, can the man, in whom the impulse to take things that do not belong to him, whether from causes innate or acquired, and is apt to become a thief, automatically and unconsciously, stop himself if he has the conscious desire to do so. Both, however, may lapse into their old conduct if their consciousness from any cause becomes clouded; that is to say, when the consciousness is not alert enough to enable them to exercise self-control.

In the course of time our varied experiences in the utilisation or repression of the impulses arising from our unconscious instincts become organised into complexes of ideas and memories, tinctured with the feelings that accompanied the original experience, and influence our conduct as a sort of intermediate barrier between our conscious and unconscious desires. They are therefore described as subconscious or, as by Freud, as preconscious. On the nature of these acquired complexes, which influence our conscious personality, the moral worth of the individual in a great measure depends. All the precepts of wisdom, wholesome examples, prudent ideas, and instructive experiences with which our youth was saturated, would be in vain if they were not organised into systems of complexes, embodied into our personality, to guide us as occasion requires. Home life, religion, politics, and other kinds of social activity form similar complexes which play a larger or smaller part in a man's life according to the amount of affect they carry, and many, if not all of them, owe their ultimate origin to one of the primary instincts. That is how we get our set ideas in the conduct of life, prejudices for good or bad in the various fields of human activity. That is the reason, for example, why a confirmed Tory and a confirmed Liberal may argue interminably, without making any progress towards a change of conviction. Only a person whose complexes are less stable or not yet fully formed on the particular subject may be convinced. What constitutes our morality becomes similarly set, and in such persons no temptation is likely to have any influence. Only in some of us, not all the instincts are so well fortified against transgression, and our weak points of armour may give way in face of a particularly tempting seduction, in which case we shall have to fall back on our quasi-morality; that is, the fear of consequences. It will be seen then, as I have pointed out before, that conduct is much more dependent on the capacity of these mental complexes to be actuated by a particular motive than on the nature of the motives themselves. The distinguishing of good and evil is a thing which is learned, and not innate, but deposited in us by our education and experience.

We inherit nothing at birth but vague tendencies, and not precise ideas or images. The tribunal of our conscience is simply the struggle, perceived by us, between our natural impulses and the moderating ideas impressed upon us in the course of our history. In other words, conscience is an acquired habit of the mind. Altogether, we may compare the individual mind to a small State in which legislative power, executive power, and judiciary power exist all in one

From what has been said so far it will be seen that morality depends to a large extent on the early education received by all of us. If the training has been defective, or vitiated by bad examples and unhealthy surroundings, the stock of ideas and complexes, if it does not favour criminal action, may be unable to withstand temptation. A child brought up to indolence or to gambling will also have no resisting power. Again, a youth who is denied opportunities of self-realisation through the narrow *milieu* in which he lives may seek gratification of his instincts in anti-social ways. Then there may be constant domestic and matrimonial difficulties, which weaken the resisting power, so that a husband or wife dos not care what happens; as, for example, if she is a nagging woman or he a drunken man. Then there are times of trouble in the life of almost all men and women, and of the best, under the influence of sorrow or business difficulty, an unhappy passion, when they may conceive some immoral or criminal plan. Every medico-psychological expert receives confidences of this kind.

These are purely psychical influences, and we have now to deal with the physical determinants. First of all there are the hereditary influences. I do not propose to discuss them, as they alone would fill a book. But I must refer to the many cases I have seen, where the parentage was absolutely sound and most of the children also perfect in character, but one only proved a degenerate. Curiously, most of these cases that have come before me were of sons of highly successful self-made men. Some of the fathers wept tears of fear of the misdeeds of their offspring becoming known.

At the present moment it is the fashion, originated by the "new" psychologists, to treat all misdemeanour as if it were purely psychical. They more or less ignore the fact that all our thoughts, emotions, and instincts are dependent on our brain, and if that organ for some reason or other is not functioning properly, our mental manifestations, and indirectly our conduct, must suffer. Thoughts come and go, and healthy, normal man can choose if he will dwell on any of them. When, however, the brain is exhausted, its blood supply accelerated or diminished, or a defective physique is weakening it, or an acquired general disease causes toxins to circulate, or the brain is under the influence of chronic alcoholism, or some point is irritated directly or indirectly, thoughts may arise and persist, thoughts of which we disapprove, but nevertheless are unable to dismiss. Such conditions may give rise to mental enfeeblement, without any apparent mental derangement. This may lead in the first instance to failure and disaster in business operations, in the man's professional activities, and in the affairs of life generally; and, as a consequence thereof, the enfeebled brain may harbour thoughts of escaping ruin by some deed which is against the law. Not infrequently such cases end by killing the family and then committing suicide.

Between the persons who are certainly insane and those who are undoubtedly sane there are a great many on or near the borderland, and it is in these cases that difficulty arises when a definite judgment has to be pronounced one way or the other. Perfect mental health is probably as rare as perfect bodily health; and it is most difficult to decide what amount of departure therefrom should be held to constitute insanity, or to confer irresponsibility. It is very difficult to perceive the motives of human action and to prove they are morbid if behind the emotional stimulus there is no delusion or intellectual deficiency. Not only is there such a state as constitutional immorality in an otherwise sound person, but in the early stages of insanity the psychosis may be slight, having only just begun, and a certain lucidity preserved, yet the patient may display a shocking degree of immorality in his feelings and conduct. In such instances the faults of character are out of proportion to the intellectual defects; yet the public, while ready to cast the stigma of insanity upon anyone who talks foolishly, hesitate to confer it upon the person who commits foolish acts.

There are no hard-and-fast lines separating sanity and insanity, soundness and unsoundness of the mind; indeed, there is no sharp division between health and disease in general, disease being nothing more than an exaggeration, or disproportion, or inharmony of normal phenomena. Whereas the general diagnosis of insanity, when once so pronounced as to necessitate certification, is in many cases so easy that it can be made by any layman, the early stages of mental unsoundness often demand all the science and skill of the most experienced observers. If it is often difficult, even in the domain of physical disease, where exact physical means for diagnosis are at hand, to decide where health changes to disease, it is still much more difficult in the psychic domain, where a standard of mental health can only be thought of as ideal, where no individual is exactly like another, and variations of thought and feeling form the majority of mankind, and even errors of the understanding and illusions of the senses, are possible within the limits of physiological activity.

At the approach of insanity the unfortunate sufferer is often conscious of a gradual loss of control over his thoughts and feelings, over his egoistic and animal instincts, but he conceals with the utmost jealousy from his relatives and friends the agony that is eating into his very soul. No doubt innumerable acts which puzzle and appear totally unaccountable to friends and strangers are the result of mental conflict hidden in the depths of the patient's mind. Of course, we all have, at some time or other, thoughts passing through our minds and feelings agitating us which, if they were expressed and indulged in, would be as wild and perhaps as frightful in their consequence as those of any madman. But the man of strong mind represses them and seeks fresh impressions from without, if he finds that aid needful. The man of weak mind yields to them, meditates on them, indulges in them, and thus they acquire fresh force, until he is totally unable to free himself from the thought or subject that haunts him. The difference between sanity and insanity consists, therefore, to a large extent, in the degree of self-control exercised.

In insanity the patient gets into a condition varying from his normal self and frequently out of relation to his environment. The alteration in the character of the subject is generally for the worse. The kindly and forbearing man becomes irritable and quarrelsome; the refined and gentlemanly man consorts with people very much beneath him, regardless of their character; the prudent man launches out in wild speculations; the previously orderly and economical man becomes confused and prodigal; the precise man exhibits carelessness and negligence; the gay man is sullen and morose; and the modest, retiring man thrusts himself forward into all kinds of society, writes long and familiar letters to persons with whom he has only a bowing acquaintance. Often there are also aversion and antipathy towards persons who previously were regarded with respect and affection—a change so painful to those towards whom it is manifested that it is usually the earliest to be noticed.

When there is an exaggeration of the natural disposition, previous faults of character and of temper manifest themselves in greater intensity, over-sensitiveness passing into melancholia, suspicion into delusion, irritable temper into uncontrollable violence, weak volition into obsession, the talkative man monopolising the conversation more completely than usual, the uxorious man becoming even more demonstrative, the egotist bragging more audaciously, the querulous man complaining more bitterly, the naturally timid and reserved man shunning society and isolating himself altogether from the companionship of his family and friends, the bold man becoming noisy and presuming, and the strictly upright person exhibiting an unhealthy exaltation of conscience respecting his moral and social duties. Of course, it is not the temporary change or exaltation of the natural characteristics which constitutes insanity; but the prolonged departure, without any adequate external cause, that is the true feature of disorder of the mind.

Now, the important fact, from the legal point of view, is that all those changes may take place without any apparent intellectual defect. The legal test of insanity is simply a test of knowledge, whereas anyone acquainted with diseases of the brain must be aware that the disorder expressed itself not only in perverted ideas, but in all sorts of perverted feelings, appetites, and instincts. The law does not embody that, but fortunately in practice it is often allowed. It is by no means unusual to find the disorders of the emotions and propensities out of all proportion greater than the disorder of the intellect, if that be disordered at all, and this is especially the case in regard to those victims of insanity who are most likely to bring themselves within reach of the criminal law. It is a common observation in lunatic asylums to find that the very persons who are most dangerous to themselves and to those about them are the most intelligent inmates of the institution.

It is very difficult to perceive the motives of human action, and to prove they are morbid, if behind the emotional stimulus there is no delusion or intellectual deficiency. It would be a great mistake to recognise insanity only when delusions can be demonstrated. Delusions are frequent, but by no means absolute, signs of insanity. In the early stage the delusion may not yet have developed, or the patient may suffer from a form of mental disorder in which no delusions occur; or he may suppress his delusions, or, even though present, they may not reach his consciousness. The sane may entertain the most outlandish false ideas, and even in this respect surpass the insane. Their error depends upon a defect of logical judgment or upon a false premise that has arisen out of uncertainty, carelessness, or embarrassment in the act of perception, such as superstition. They can be argued out of their delusion. A delusion of the insane, on the other hand, is a symptom of brain disorder, and therefore logic and reasoning are powerless against it.

To establish a defence on the ground of insanity in an English law-court it must be clearly proved that at the time of committing the act the person accused was labouring under such a defect of reason from disease of the mind as not to know the nature and quality of the act; or, if he did know it, that he did not know he was doing what was wrong. We have already shown that the grades of responsibility cannot be standardised in degrees of intelligence. The mere knowing of the difference between right and wrong is of little value in itself—a child may know it, and yet not have sufficient strength of mind to prompt him to right conduct. Reason cannot always control the desire when it knows its good or bad quality and can appreciate the right or wrong of it. Insane persons may know when they are doing wrong; indeed, whether they give themselves up at once to the police or try to make their escape, they prove by this action that they know they have done wrong. We repeat, the main difference between sanity and insanity is the ability of self-control. The sane criminal will not, and the insane criminal cannot, exercise self-control. In the eyes of the law, the ideal madman acts without motives or acts from insane motives; and therefore if a rational motive can be found for the criminal offence, such as lust, rage, greed, or any other passion, there is no ground to allege insanity; or, at any rate, no ground to allege exemption from responsibility, by reason of insanity. The insane have the same feelings and passions as those who are not insane, but they do not exercise restraint to the same extent as normal persons. It is the unstable condition of their brain centres which allows action to take place upon impulse—or even with premeditation—which a healthy state of the brain would have enabled them to resist. Most of the insane know when they are doing wrong, are able to distinguish right from wrong, but they have not the power of choosing right from wrong. They are conscious of what they contemplate doing, but have not the power to stop the brain machinery; they lack the self-control. Especially if the act recurs again and again, even the sternest lawyer should be suspicious of the mental state of the accused; but I have before me the judgment on a case of exhibitionism, in which I was interested, which was embellished by the judge with the remark that the accused was the most disgusting villain that had ever come before him.

Taking even sane persons, it must be apparent to the most ordinary observer that the majority of authors of violent and reckless crimes, especially homicide, manslaughter and serious assaults, are under such influence of passion as to obscure reason and reflection for the time being, and that they are not thinking at all at that moment of the consequences of their acts, or that they are doing wrong. Whether a jealous husband shoots his wife's lover to vindicate his own honour, as sometimes happens in France, or a burglar stabs a policeman in order to prevent himself being arrested, as sometimes happens in England, each may be, at the time of the act, incapable of distinguishing right from wrong. In the first case the thirst for revenge, in the second the desire for liberty, completely obscures the moral sense.

Insanity is not capable of close definition. It cannot always be proved by a question of facts, but often only by inference from facts, and what a judge and jury would infer from the same facts is often at variance. The duty of the medical expert, as a witness called either by the prosecution or defence, is to elucidate, for the assistance of the court, the state of the accused's mind as it appeared to him at the time of the examination, and as it might be deemed to have been at the time of the commission of the offence; and it is the lawyer's business to determine responsibility as nearly as he can in accordance with the facts the doctor supplied to him. The conditions of responsibility have never been more clearly defined as by the late Dr. Mercier, namely: In order to be responsible the accused must have willed the act, intended the harm, and desired primarily his own gratification; the act must have been done on inadequate provocation; and the accused must know and appreciate the circumstances in which the act was done. If any of these factors be wanting, responsibility is impaired or abolished.

If experts confined themselves to facts, conflict of medical evidence would often be avoided. The question of sanity has to be decided chiefly in cases of sexual crime, larceny, manslaughter, and most frequently in cases of murder. The decision often presents difficulties, which too frequently manifest themselves in the courts in a manner which does not impress the lawyers or the public with the value of medical testimony. The conflict of testimony arises partly from the fact that the expert tries to make out a case for the side which engages him.

Insanity is often a matter of opinion, and cannot be proved even by post-mortem methods. Practically nothing is known of the *mental* functions of the brain; therefore no expert can give evidence as to cerebral disease, unless the offender is actually insane, epileptic or a drunkard, and known as such to others. To take only one aspect of insanity, which I have brought forward so much in this book: head injuries. The effects of localised lèsions of the brain have never received much attention, even by experts. In my work *In Search of the Soul* I have shown on the strength of hundreds of cases that according to the locality affected so a man may develop symptoms of kleptomania, homicidal tendencies, immoderate or perverse sexual activity, or other immoral disposition. The neglect of these observations has as a consequence that a man might have, for example, a syphilitic gumma in one of these brain areas, and yet pass as sound. In one such case I saved the man in face of considerable opposition. Two years later the man died, and my diagnosis was confirmed at the post-mortem examination. True, these irritative lesions and these poisons, whether syphilitic or other, do not suffice to make moral offenders, without consideration of the inherited mental disposition; but they constitute an admirable state of predisposition towards every sort of formidable exaggeration, and all the acts of beasts of prey.

If there is still doubt as to the importance of

head injuries, there is none as to the importance of epilepsy. Every layman knows an epileptic if he sees him in convulsions; but it is not sufficiently known that an epileptic after the fit may still remain for a time in a state of clouded consciousness, and that the fit itself may be replaced by a paroxysm of mania, and that in both states actions may be performed innocent, immoral, or criminal, of which the epileptic has no or only a confused recollection. I have published in the work mentioned the history of two cases of epileptics, proved to be so on medical testimony, who were found guilty of murder. In one case the Court of Appeal quashed the sentence, in the other the man was hanged. I have also shown that a number of similar cases were cured both of their fits and their homicidal tendencies by surgical operation. But so long as medical experts have preconceived notions on the subject and are unwilling to examine the evidence put before them, it cannot be expected that a criminal court will attach any value to the defence of epilepsy.

As a rule it should not be difficult to decide between a case of murder and one of insane homicide. The manner in which the murderer sets himself to the commission of his crime, as well as his subsequent conduct, is very different from the proceedings of the madman. The former often has accomplices; he commences with premeditation, lays a plan beforehand, chooses time, place, and circumstances adapted to the perpetration of the deed, and generally has contrived some method of escape after the catastrophe. He always studies concealment and personal safety, and when there is danger of detection uses all possible despatch to escape the punishment due to his crime. Moreover, the murderer seldom sheds more blood than is necessary for the attainment of his object. All these particulars are reversed in the madman. He has either no motive or he acts under a motive which, to a sane mind, would be quite inadequate. He has no accomplices, he rarely communicates his purpose to others, he rushes on his victim as if driven by a sudden impulse, seizes whatever weapon chance throws in his way, and sometimes seems to be excited powerfully to the attempt by the sight of implements fitted to his purpose. He lays no plan for escape, and seldom attempts it after perpetrating the act. When genuine delusions are present, the murderer is often only too willing to narrate the circumstances, to explain his grievances, and to justify his conduct. By the courtesy of governors of prisons I have made studies of various murderers; but I have never been called as a witness in a case of murder, though I had been engaged on two occasions for the defence. Both these accused committed suicide in their cells before the date of their trial.

The question is whether a person who is shown to have been temporarily insane, or suffering from masked epilepsy, or clouded consciousness from some other cause, would not be better if he received the due punishment for his deed. The arguments against such punishment are all based on the idea of retrospective and retributive justice. Of course, we cannot balance a certain amount of wrong-doing by a certain amount of pain to be inflicted. It is otherwise, however, if we regard punishment as wholly prospective, as an element of motive for the future. Even the insane can appreciate prospective punishment and shape their conduct accordingly. But by far the best examples we get in the animal world. It is natural for a cat or dog to steal, they are following only their instincts, but repeated hidings leave such an impression that the domestic pet will refrain in the future from stealing, or at least hesitate in the act, and experience a sort of sense of guilt if it has done wrong, as shown by its slinking away after the act. A man who has intercourse with any woman he has just met may become the victim of venereal disease—he has to take the consequences of his folly; if he seduces another man's daughter, he must also take the consequences, whatever his state of mind may have been. I think it was Mr. Justice Stephen who said at a discussion on Crime and Insanity that if the man cannot help committing a crime, the law cannot help sending him to prison. But it may be argued, Is it not unjust, in the face of my own evidence of certain brain derangements leading to criminal acts, to punish such a criminal? First of all this will depend on the individual case, but speaking as a physician to physicians, I should say our primary duty is not to save the individual man from punishment, but to study such brain disorders and *prevent* them leading to crime.

We are all swayed by motives, and if the fear of punishment were abolished, it would give greater licence to all evil-doers. The experience of the leading authorities makes it clear that even the insane man is the better for being held responsible, if he is capable of any appreciation of cause and effect. He realises that the whole style of the treatment he receives and the amount of liberty and enjoyment allowed him depend entirely on the degree of control he exercises over himself. So long as a man is capable of foreseeing, or of being taught to foresee, the consequences of his acts, these consequences ought to be allowed their full weight in the composition of his motives.

At the same time there might be graduated punishment, especially in the case of murder, not depending on the criminal act, but on the individuality of the criminal; and where there is some evidence of brain disease or injury the evil-doer should be confined in prison hospital until such time as surgeons have succeeded in restoring him. Certainly, no criminal suspected of mental disorder should be hanged, for insanity may be discovered after conviction, though not admitted at the trial, and the stigma of crime will be attached unnecessarily to the offender and his family.

The Law recognises only two classes of criminals: the sane, fully responsible; and the sane, irresponsible. But, as we have shown, there is a large intermediate class of congenital moral defectives, who have been the shame and terror of their families from early childhood, who know fully well what they are doing and on whom punishment has no effect. We may call them morally weak-minded, degenerates, or by any other name; only, one fact must be recognised, that is, that *they are not insane.* What is to be done with them? That is the problem on which public opinion is divided, but which will have to be solved sooner or later.

CHAPTER XII

TREATMENT OF MORAL FAILINGS

THE task of a medical psychologist falls into two parts: a practical and a theoretical. He must, in the first place, try to understand the soul-life of his patients in its deepest recesses, while he lays bare the hidden aim towards which all the actions and psychical deliverances of the patient are unconsciously directed. He does not deal, of course, as I have already said, with the professional criminal, who makes crime his vocation, and follows it as a trade or profession. The moral offenders that come before him belong to the domain of mental pathology. The misconduct or immoral disposition is often a very different one from the initial cause, which the expert discovers on probing deeper. For example, the kleptomaniac may be a drug taker or a fundamentally lazy person; again, that laziness may be due to constitutional weakness which can be treated medically, or it may be due to moral deficiency for which psychotherapy, including the systematic re-education of character, may be necessary. Again, the offence for which he or his friends consult the physician, though said to be the first delinquency, may have been going on for some time. It need not be the same offence. Many of the morally defective persons start as gross liars.

Our first duty, before we attempt any psychical treatment, is to remember that though the symptoms are mental, the causes are not necessarily so; they may be physical. Apart from any actual disease there may be a lowered tone of the nervous system, and no psychical treatment will have any effect until the vital energy is uplifted. I have known doctors to resent the application of physical measures by the psychotherapist, protesting that they did not send the patient for physical treatment; and I had to explain to them that to impose psychotherapeutics before attending to the constitutional deficiency would mean either failure or a treatment more prolonged than the patients could afford. The neglect of this measure accounts to a great extent for the complaint by some that psychotherapy is followed by relapses.

When anyone is said to fail in life because his character is indolent, apathetic, wanting in moral energy and will, the failure is often ascribed to moral causes and blame imputed to him, whereas the truth may be that his constitution lacks the requisite vital energy which he cannot infuse into himself by merely wishing it, as M. Coué, of Nancy, tells him to do. The heart may be weak, the circulation languid, the digestion feeble, and the nervous system below par, and without being actually ill, he may keep himself going only by fits and starts; that is, by occasional great efforts. The lowered vitality may give him a craving for stimulants, and many a delinquent starts as a temporary alcoholic. Sometimes certain emotions are over-active, and by the galvanometer it has been shown that they alter the electrical conductivity of the body. On the other hand, we can by galvanic currents properly applied alter the intensity of the emotions, and, what is more, increase the nervous energy.

To me the size and shape of the head is always a great revelation. I have tried to convey such knowledge to my learned friends, but the head continues to be of no interest to them. Even a considerable deformity is left unobserved. One cannot be surprised, therefore, that there is not even a theory in existence as to what constitutes a good head or a bad one. That is why the examination of head injury is so much neglected, and the effects ignored. This is not the place to discuss the subject. All I wish to do is to record my observations for the benefit of any future investigator, who will find all the evidence in the oft-mentioned work of mine, *In Search of the Soul*. I have shown, among other things:

that persons may become thieves after injury to the anterior-superior temporal region;

that they may suffer from increased irascibility and commit acts of violence and homicide after injury to the lower temporal region;

that they may become suspicious and develop delusions of persecution after injury to the posterior or temporal region;

that they may be guilty of sexual offences after blows on the lower occipital region;

that they may get depressed, melancholic and suicidal after injury to the parietal bones;

and that in injury to the frontal bones there may be intellectual changes together with moral lapses from lack of inhibitory power, the offence varying according to the person's natural tendencies, which then become exaggerated.

Of course, in all these cases the brain must have received damage in the particular locality. When these brain areas are affected by other causes—inflammation, new growths, etc.—the same symptoms follow. Whenever surgical treatment was undertaken in the cases I have quoted, the patient recovered. While I am writing this (March 11th) the medical papers have arrived reporting two more cases in confirmation of my localisations, in which, by a strange procedure, the injuries were not discovered by direct observation of the head, but by a confession in the process of treatment by psycho-analysis. Surgical treatment again cured the patients.

Having attended to the physical condition of the patient and excluded all organic trouble, we then proceed to what is commonly called suggestion treatment, in which must be included all the possible psycho-therapeutic measures. Personally, I refuse to confine myself to any one of them. I have shown in my book on *Hypnotism and Suggestion* what wonderful and lasting results can be achieved by the application of hypnotism, provided only we do not limit ourselves to the methods which became so popular through Dr. Bernheim, of Nancy. When hypnotism was accepted by the profession and was for a time fashionable, its practitioners claimed that they could hypnotise about 90 per cent. of their patients. I have never found it so. Nor is a state of hypnosis or actual sleep necessary for therapeutic purposes, only for the manifestation of certain higher phenomena, which are of interest to the scientist and psychologist only. All that is needed is a sort of passive, somnolent condition, a mental state of calm and physical and mental relaxation, which causes the patient to become receptive to the impressions that we wish to make upon his or her mind. This passive state simply means the partial suspension of the functions of the conscious state of the mind for the time being, for the purpose of allowing the subconscious mind to receive impressions and to act upon them. As is well known, hypnotism is induced by the subject himself, and not by the operator. Now it sometimes happens that by the method here described a patient does go right off, in which case suggestions can be made more easily. But as a rule he keeps wide awake, mentally at least, but his whole body seems to him as if it were asleep; that is to say, it feels heavy and the limbs require an effort to be moved. That is the condition which I find the best for patients whose troubles are more or less serious and of long standing and who therefore can no longer be treated by the simpler form of psychotherapy, that of persuasion alone.

Influenced by the public performances of showmen, people regard hypnotism as something uncanny, and modern psychoanalysts are doing their best to increase their prejudice against it. But I can assure the unbiassed reader that if a person can be hypnotised properly, i.e. deeply—very few can—it is a blessing to him, for in that case he may be certain of a speedy recovery. I refer, of course, to the ordinary functional ailments; but even the evil-doer—the chronic drunkard, inveterate liar and thief, and the sexual pervert can be treated by this method, and I have done so successfully in many cases. Of course, I have also had my failures, but I can explain these. Sometimes the patient's own doctor insists on hypnotism, whether the malady is suitable for it or not, and we are always willing to try; at other times the patient asks too much, as when he expects to be cured with one or two treatments. For instance, quite a number of patients have come to me soaked in alcohol and hoped that by some mysterious procedure I would send them to sleep and that when they woke and walked home they would be able to ignore every public-house on their way. Even that I have done; but such a case is miraculous, and miracles occur rarely, otherwise they would not be miracles.

A number of objections to hypnotism as a method of treatment have been raised by the latest psychoanalytic school:

1. It is said that after hypnotic treatment there is a tendency to relapse or for other symptoms to arise. I deny this absolutely. Relapses occur only if the patient has been imperfectly hypnotised; when the wrong suggestions have been made; when the re-education of the character has been neglected; and certainly when the operator, like the modern psychoanalyst, neglects to treat the physical condition and state of the brain and nervous system of the patient. Freud asserts that "the method is a failure in certain cases." Probably it was so with him; that is why he invented the method of psychoanalysis. But psychoanalysis is not a panacea either, and of what method can it be said that it is free from failure? It is said that the pathogenetic idea at the root of the trouble is not dealt with by the hypnotist. Possibly the writer who raised this objection, and was himself a hypnotist before he became converted to psychoanalysis, did not remove the pathogenetic idea, but he has no right to affirm that others neglect doing so.

2. It is said that hypnotism makes the patient

dependent on the doctor. This again is untrue. Whatever the patient does, he does himself. The operator adds nothing but strength of will and stability of character; and he takes nothing away, except the source of mischief in the patient's mental organisation. I even remove the very suggestibility which makes certain people such easy subjects for hypnotism and makes them susceptible to relapses by the suggestion of contrary ideas. Many years ago a lady consulted me for acute neuritis, for which her local doctor had given her daily injections of morphia. She wanted to be hypnotised. I succeeded instantaneously, and all the pains disappeared. She had another treatment the same week, still feeling well. But when she came the week after, she professed to be "worse than ever." On cross-examination I elicited the information that one day her doctor had called to inquire why she stopped the injections, and, on being told of my success, he replied: "Hypnotism is humbug; your neuritis is just the same." Whereupon the pains returned. Ever since I follow the method of "de-hypnotisation" to prevent my patients being influenced by counter-suggestions.

3. Freud declares that another objection he has to hypnotism is the "fear of the transference of sexual feeling to the person of the physician." This objection does not come well from Freud, for, as he himself acknowledges, there is in his own method of psychoanalysis invariably a transference of that

nature. I have never experienced such a thing in my own practice, but I can well imagine it to take place sometimes, for it is by no means a rare occurrence for a girl to fall in love with her doctor, even when she is not hypnotised.

Mental analysis can, and should be, practised by every medical psychologist. But psychoanalytic treatment is rarely practical, for, according to the best authorities, it requires the attendance of a patient "for one hour a day six times a week for probably a year." For the poorer and middle classes a lengthy psychoanalysis is therefore inapplicable. There are three methods in use:

1. The "free association" method in which the patient is encouraged to speak freely whatever comes into his mind "no matter how painful or even disgusting any revived memories may be."

2. The "word association" method, when the patient is not allowed to talk of his own, but is given in succession different words, and has to tell the physician the first idea that comes into his mind. It is obvious that the word selected may act "suggestively" on the patient, and, considering that the patient's entire life has to be gone through, it is apparent that he may fill in details with his own fancy, when he can no longer remember them.

3. The "dream analysis" method, i.e. the discovery of the symbolic meaning of the various

ideas occurring in a dream. Considering that " every dream is the realisation of some infantile sexual desire " and that almost all dreams are " symbolical from a sexual standpoint " (a whole list of words, objects, situations, being appended to some of the works of Freudians, all signifying sex organs, sex desires, and normal and abnormal sexual acts), it would seem there are none other than erotic dreams.

When a patient has nothing to say, or hesitates with his reply, the physician knows he has touched upon the vulnerable point. Now, to avoid being accused of misinterpretation, let me quote an authority : " When this resistance is overcome, the situation reveals itself as one in which the patient is found *to have selected the physician as a suitable object on which to lavish intense feelings of affection (or dislike). When the analyst is a man and the patient a woman, this affection may have every appearance of normal love and is often maintained by the patient to be such*, although the circumstances of the treatment and the attitude of the physician have provided no justification for such a development. *The situation arises regularly in every successful analysis*, and although at one time it was thought that it might be only an unfortunate accidental occurrence which interfered with the therapeutic work, it is now known to be not merely an inevitable accompaniment of the analytic process, but the necessary foundation of its successful prosecution." (T. W. Mitchell: *The Psychology of Medicine*, pp. 157 and 158.)

From the above it is evident that psychoanalytic treatment is a risky procedure for the physician, and dangerous to the patient if undertaken by a layman. There will have to be considerable modification of its methods before it can be generally applied; before all, there must be a recognition that the sex instinct, although a primary and all-engrossing one, is not the only instinct which may be repressed. It would be a pity if a reaction set in against Freud's psychology and his important contributions to the understanding of normal and abnormal mental life, because of the misguided zeal of some of his followers who insist on seeing glaring sex manifestations everywhere, when such eminent disciples of Freud as Jung and Adler have given up that view, and many of our British Freudians are not even practising the methods of which they speak so highly.

As I have said already, we do not depend on hypnotism. All that is necessary for purposes of treatment is the production of a passive state, to make the patient more concentrated and indirectly more impressionable to our advice and treatment. My first efforts are directed to discover what are the patient's most active inherited propensities and emotions, what are his acquired sentiments and complexes, whether any of them are repressed or unrepressed, whether they are properly co-ordinated and controlled, and whether they are grouped round some dominating passion or aim, and what complexes, habits, or conflicts are responsible for the patient's troubles and misconduct. It is not the repressed psychical event that is important, but the discovery of the underlying motive. All the active propensities and sentiments may be repressed, and not only "libido sexualis" to which the Freudian school has attached exclusive significance.

Mental conflict is a frequent cause of delinquency. The finer the emotional qualities, the greater the suffering from mental conflicts. A great variety of misconduct may arise from them, ranging from the sustained bad behaviour of childhood to deeds of actual crime, including obstinacy, destructiveness, truancy, vagrancy, stealing, forgery, sexual offences, injury to others. It is remarkable that some of these misdoers are not carrying out their own keenest desires; their misdeeds are, as it were, "forced by something in themselves, not of themselves"; they involve no pleasure.

Mental analysis is of great value because the real concealed source of the delinquency often has no obvious connection with the nature of the delinquent act. Careful diagnosis is absolutely essential, for in many cases the misconduct of which a man is accused is not the cause of his going wrong and is not the condition which requires treatment. I have known an employee steal and defraud to pay for his school fees, having in his spare hours started study for a profession.

Having taken stock of the patient's mind and assessed its various contents at their proper value, the next step in a comprehensive psychotherapy is that of re-education. We have to bring about a readjustment, some sought-for and desirable reorganisation of the individual in respect of his inner and outer experience; to assist him, as well as may be, in his efforts, hitherto frustrated, towards the consummation of a more harmonious adaptation to his social and physical environment; in other words, the reconciliation of the patient with reality. We have to teach him orderly thought and controlled emotion, i.e. mental discipline and self-control. Mere exploration of his mental contents without such re-education is bound to prove a failure.

Often we have to supply that moral education which has been neglected in youth. Many of our boys and girls, when they have finished their education, are totally untrained in the power to deal with the world, and cannot guard themselves against the "business" capacities of those with whom they come in contact, not to speak of the slyness of those who prey upon the ignorant. Many a lad who might possibly have done well had he received practical training in the art of social existence becomes a "waster" or fails otherwise in his career. He has not learned worldly wisdom in the struggle with those eager "to do him," and he is ignorant of his own powers and weaknesses and how to regulate them.

In order to help the patient towards self-realisation and self-perfection, we have to introduce new aims and supply new motives for right action. We must evoke ideals and the impulse to pursue them, and make them so attractive to the patient that they become embodied in the processes of conduct. Of course, the ideals must be practical, not Utopian. By the implanting of new ideals we tap the potential subconscious reserve-energy of the patient, bring about a re-association and synthesis of the dissociated mental systems underlying his immoral inclinations, and restore self-confidence, confidence in his own abilities to do the work for which he is gifted. Altogether, we have to correct the faults of the early education, for it must be remembered that even congenital immorality need not manifest itself, if the child is properly trained. There is no character which has not some redeeming points, and we must fit the training to the child, not the child to the training.

The mental pathologist is a luxury for the atavistic offspring of the rich. He saves them from becoming vicious or criminal, or at least from being arraigned before a criminal court. But what about the poor? Why should there not be a scientific inquiry into the causes of their delinquency, an inquiry into their nature and nurture? Birmingham is the only city in Great Britain that employs a medical psychologist for that purpose. Why should not a medical psychologist be called in to supervise a form of punishment which shall be not only a discipline but a training, at least in the case of first offenders? It is much to the credit of Court Missionaries and Probation Officers who have done me the honour to seek my advice at a purely nominal fee about the causes of the delinquency and the best means of training the young offenders entrusted to their charge. But I should like to see a sort of mental hospital or Receiving House connected with our criminal courts, where all doubtful and remediable cases could be sent, in the first instance, for report to the presiding judge. That the question of insanity in a case of murder should be left for decision to the wisdom of a jury seems to me outrageous. No doubt the judge sees to it that justice is done, but even the judge cannot be wiser than the experts, and he often differs from them. Every murderer who is suspected of insanity or of malingering insanity should be sent to the proposed Observation Hospital, whose expert staff would examine and watch the accused, and send a report of the facts observed to the judge before trial. Let the law then do the rest as it thinks fit.

In milder offences, too, proper minute psychological certificates of the whole mentality of the criminal, inherited and acquired, would be better than the present customary references as to character. I am afraid, however, fewer would escape their penalty than do now. For it is human nature to help the man who is down in his luck, even if he be a criminal, so long as we are not the injured party.

Just as the well-to-do seek the mental pathologist, so, if we had observation hospitals, would the poor bring their misguided boys and girls; and if thus the skilled investigation were carried out while the delinquency was yet only potential, the stigma of guilt and arrest might be avoided and the community would gain by the prevention of criminal acts. Certainly every industrial school and reformatory should have its psychological expert. Uninvestigated offenders are the most expensive luxury that any community can indulge in. I would plead for the most careful medico-psychological study of delinquents, not only from motives of humanity and justice to the delinquent, but for the prophylaxis of future offences and the protection of society.

INDEX